T5-ACP-668

SABBATH
peace

SABBATH peace

A BOOK OF MEDITATIONS

MOSHE A. BRAUN

JASON ARONSON INC.
Northvale, New Jersey
Jerusalem

This book was set in 13 pt. Souvenir by Alpha Graphics of Pittsfield, New Hampshire.

Copyright © 1997 by Moshe A. Braun

10 9 8 7 6 5 4 3 2 1

All rights reserved. Printed in the United States of America. No part of this book may be used or reproduced in any manner whatsoever without written permission from Jason Aronson Inc. except in the case of brief quotations in reviews for inclusion in a magazine, newspaper, or broadcast.

Library of Congress Cataloging-in-Publication Data
Brown, Moshe.
    Sabbath peace / Moshe A. Braun.
        p.   cm.
    ISBN 0-7657-9957-X
    1. Sabbath—Meditations. 2. Hasidism. 3. Cabala. I. Title.
BM685.B74   1997
296.4'1—dc21   97-26352

Manufactured in the United States of America. Jason Aronson Inc. offers books and cassettes. For information and catalog write to Jason Aronson Inc., 230 Livingston Street, Northvale, NJ 07647.

לזכר נשמת
שרה בת מרדכי ע"ה

This book is dedicated to Sarah Bas Mordechai - affectionately known as Shaindily Babi by her large extended family. The name was coined by one of her small granddaughters many years ago and it stayed with her to the end.

She was royal with the manner of aristocracy, yet humble; small in stature yet clothed in dignity and grandeur - every inch a queen. Babi brought us love, kindness, and healing, a refined use of language and penetrating wisdom. We never heard her criticize nor ever utter a harsh word. She guided us with quiet discussion and wholehearted interest. Babi's faith and trust in the Almighty were unshakable. She was over a hundred, having lived through two World Wars with great suffering and loss. Yet, her prayers remained as innocent and sincere as a child's.

Shaindily Babi was the thread of continuity, connecting us with those of generations past. She showed us how women of yesteryear ushered in the Shabbos - the way she did. With prayer book in hand, tearfully beseeching God for the safety of all His children.

Her loving memory is a blessing for us, and may it guide us always.

Contents

Acknowledgments vii
Introduction ix

1 A Gift 1

2 Infinite Light 17

3 Holiness 33

4 Spiritual Warmth 49

5 In God's Presence 57

6 The Torah 85

7 Divine Rest 97

8 Remembering 119

9 Perfection 137

10 Peace 169

Traditional Sabbath Observance 183

Acknowledgments

I would like to thank my dear wife Leah for being the pillar of strength for the family both in good times and hard times. I watched her ushering in the Sabbath hundreds of times with tearful prayers for the well-being of the family and the world. May her merit be a tent of peace over our children: Zevy, Pessie, and Chevele; Shaindy, Sruly, Surala, Shmuel Zevy, Gitty, and Dovid Yitzchok Isaak; Mutty, Gitty, Yisroel Reuven, Chayala, and Yaakov Akiva; Chavy, Daniel, Yisroel, and Yehuda; Chaya Yitty and Yosef Yehudah Yitzchok Isaac. May they all live to experience Sabbath peace.

Introduction

Heaven and earth, and all their components, were thus completed. With the seventh day, God finished all the work that He had done. He thus ceased on the seventh day from all the work that He had been doing. God blessed the seventh day, and He declared it to be holy, for it was on this day that God ceased from all the work that He had been creating so that it would continue to function.
—Genesis 2:1-3

We honor the seventh day not only as God's day of rest, but also for the fact that God created the world. In observing its holiness with our cessation of work, we witness to all mankind that God is master and ruler. It is, therefore, higher than all other commandments. If one honors the Sabbath, even if he is an idol worshiper, he will attain forgiveness, while one who desecrates the Sabbath is as if he dishonored the entire Torah.

Sabbath is the fulcrum, the center around which all of Judaism revolves. It is our holiest day, declaring unequivocally that God is master and we, His servants, receive independence only through Him.

It is the day, once, each and every week, to reorient our life's goals and pursuits to those of God's purpose and to be in harmony with it; to cease, stop, remain still, in total serenity and peace; to end all disharmony, dissonance, and discord, and allow tranquility to prevail.

Consider the cosmic importance of the Sabbath in man's life: at no time can anything be so important that one cannot stop doing it from sundown to sundown. By establishing a threshold of pursuit, it touches the very root of mankind's values and civilization. It is a weekly "mid-course correction," setting him straight from days of aimless stumbling.

Think of the influence of the Sabbath on those who observe it and on the rest of humanity. Sabbath declares that one cannot become enslaved to a person or a project. He must rest 1 day of the 7. Not only he, but every member of his household. Not only the humans, but even the animals.

This was a radical and revolutionary idea in ancient times, with Pharaoh complaining about the "laziness" of his enslaved Hebrews. We read words of derision and mockery heaped upon the Israelites by the Greeks and Romans for their refusal to work 7 days a week! They were ridiculed also for their equating the treatment of animals to those of people and allowing their horses, oxen, and cows to rest 1 day a week. Outrageous!

Introduction

Sabbath is truly revolutionary, and its observance by the early Hebrews was thousands of years ahead of its time. Is it any wonder that Jews were at the forefront in the battle against inequality of workers and the working class? They were the organizers of the first unions, protecting the rights of workers and improving their working conditions. They also pioneered and organized protection of animals.

Sabbath sets us apart as a holy people, with the opportunity to digest other cultures by choosing the holy sparks therein and rejecting the chaff.

It was surely the ultimate gift given to the Israelites for neither reason nor merit. Thus, it is witness to the intrinsic connection between God and His people. Evil can conspire day and night for 6 days and nights to separate us from God, but to no avail. Come Sabbath, and we are just as close to Him as ever.

We all need to be reminded of the magnitude of its importance, and there is no better way than by learning from those who delved into its beauty and fathomed its significance. Those are the teachers who devoted their lives to raising the spiritual consciousness of their followers. From among them I have chosen the Chasidic masters, who, in my opinion, have revealed, illuminated, and clarified the deep secrets and symbolism of the Torah. They based their teachings on the kabbala, which contains the innermost secrets of our relationship with God, the Creation, and the meaning of Torah verses. Their teachings simplify by using comparisons, analogies, and parables. In that way, even an unschooled person can understand them.

Chasidic teachings touch not only your mind, but also your emotions. Therefore, they relate to one's personal life and existential struggles.

I have based my writing on the teachings of a preeminent Chasidic master, the famous Rabbi Yehudah Aryeh Leib Alter, the second leader of the Chasidic dynasty of Gur. He was born to the first Gerer Rebbe, Rabbi Avraham Mordechai Alter, who was the only son of the Chidushei Ha'rim, in Warsaw, on the eve of Rosh Chodesh Iyar, in 1847. Orphaned as a young boy, he was educated by his grandfather, who was one of the greatest Torah sages of that time. Even at that young age, he learned Torah with great diligence, 18 hours a day. To visiting scholars, his grandfather would say, "Look at my grandson how he studies Torah!" When the grandfather passed away, the Chasidim wanted to appoint him as the next Gerer Rebbe. Being merely 19 years old, he refused and instead went as a pupil to the Rebbe of Aleksander. Four years later, the Rebbe of Aleksander passed away, and again the Chasidim urged him to take on the yoke of leadership. This time he accepted. He molded Gur as a center of Chasidut, attracting tens of thousands of followers from all over Europe. His commentaries on the Talmud made him renowned as a great Torah scholar as

Introduction

well as a brilliant leader. For more than 30 years, he counseled his followers to live with fervent devotion to the Torah, both in study and deed. In 1905, at the age of 57, a few days before he passed away, he had written the last of his written words, "Lips of truth, *S'fas Emes*, stand firm forever" (Proverbs 12:19). And because they were the last words of his earthly sojourn, his sons chose them as a lasting tribute and named all his writings *S'fas Emes*.

The *S'fas Emes* on the Torah, which is the basis for this book, has a uniquely deep and exciting approach to interpreting its verses and topics. Besides their depth, they encompass a wide spectrum of quotations, analogies, and comparisons from the Talmud, Midrash, and Zohar. His teachings are constantly bursting with new ideas in every sentence, phrase, and word. He is like a brook, endlessly bubbling forth, that tastes differently each time you drink from it.

It is hoped that with this book you will gain an understanding of Chasidic thought and a glimpse of the kabbala; that you will pause in your busy life and take note of this marvelous gift from God to mankind: the Sabbath.

1
A Gift

The Gift

Anyone can stop work on the Sabbath,
but only God can give rest. It is a gift.

To Receive

One who receives a gift is happy,
but also embarrassed. It reminds him that
he is lacking and imperfect. Sabbath is also
a gift, yet no one is embarrassed to receive
it. It is not given because we are lacking,
but to elevate us beyond limitations
and divisions. It is the ultimate
unity from the highest sphere.

work

First, man must prepare vessels during the six workdays. Then he receives the Sabbath.

---

a field

The world is a barren field. Sabbath is fertile and ready for planting. If we are powerless as a field, God plants His light in us.

---

giving all away

Those who give everything away receive everything in return. He who gives away the results of his work of the six workdays receives the entire gift of the Sabbath.

---

out of many, one

During the holidays, the union of the many hearts causes holiness to descend. On the Sabbath, the unity is a gift.

unified soul

All work that makes a significant change is forbidden on the Sabbath: plowing, planting, reaping, cooking, and carrying from one domain to another. All of them are accomplished with the three life forces: the breath of life, the spirit, and soul of man. On Sabbath, however, man receives the "soul of the soul" from a realm beyond material existence. And, therefore, if he were to do work with the help of that lofty soul, its energy would remain in the fragments of this broken world. Its unity would also be broken and lose its spiritual strength.

To Eat

The one who worked hard on Sabbath eve will eat on Sabbath. Not as a result of his work, rather as a gift.

The stone

There is the well, the source of all blessing, and the stone, the illusion of difficulty, covering it. On the Sabbath, the stone is removed, and all who desire drink freely.

To Fix

Man must fix all of nature, even his own.
Some of his brokenness, however,
is beyond natural effort. To that end,
the gift of the Sabbath is granted. It is
beyond the natural world, and in her each
comes to its ultimate perfection.

To Be an Angel

Angels are created for a specific task and
are static in their spiritual level. Man,
on the other hand, is dynamic and can
strive to attain the level of angels.
That place is the Sabbath.

The World to Come

The purpose of a vessel is to contain that
which is placed into it. And man, too,
is a vessel for the light of God. And
although unrefined in the present state,
he will be fit in the World to Come.
The Sabbath is from that world and is
received to show our worthiness and
chosenness for the World to Come.

A Gift

worthy

If we are worthy, we can experience
God giving the Sabbath to us.
And if not, is it worth it?

The vessel

When we stand in awe of God, we are
humble, empty vessels to receive
His blessings. The Sabbath, a reminder of
God the creator, moves us to awe,
thus preparing us for her blessings.
The ultimate gift, peace, also comes only if
preceded by awe. It can be derived
from the word, Jerusalem, *Yerushalayim*:
yorei, awe, *sholem*, peace. When we
are in awe of God, we have peace.

The womb

The dead do not produce offspring.
Thus, renewal and blessing come only
from the Sabbath. It is the womb for
the life of the six workdays.

Beyond Reason

Just as the covenant between God and
the Jewish people is independent of
their deeds, so, too, is the Sabbath.
It is totally a gift.

Sustenance

Sustenance in the weekdays is according
to man's work; and, therefore is decreed
during the judgment on New Year's day.
But what he receives on Sabbath is from
spheres beyond the natural realm; and,
therefore, all of man's needs for the
Sabbath are beyond judgment and are
given with total kindness.

Seeds

God plants many gifts into every heart.
When Sabbath arrives and concealment is
uncovered, the heart's secrets also appear.
And that which we merely yearned for
can then become reality.

A Gift of Unity

The Jewish nation, as a whole, possesses unity. Those who are not impeded by sin easily join the *klal*, the collective. When the Sabbath comes, a spiritual unity descends with it; and even the sinners are swept along in its wave of togetherness.

The Godly Portion

Who is rich? He who is happy with his share. Those who return a portion to God can rejoice with the rest. Similarly, we give away one of the week's days to God, the Sabbath, and the other six, are for our work.

The Well

God grants the Sabbath peace and also grants its preparation: the well and the path to the well.

Receiving

By preparing to receive and then receiving
the Sabbath, we get its blessing.

Treasure

After seeking a lost object with anxiety
and great effort, finding it is no great joy.
Finding a treasure, although without dread,
is cause for celebration: and that
is the Sabbath.

To Accept

If we accept the six workdays as the will
of God, we are worthy to enjoy
the full gift of the Sabbath.

Infinite Blessing

The six days of creation are the vessel
for God's blessing. The Sabbath is the
blessing itself and beyond any vessel.
Only those who become infinite
through the Torah have the capacity
for fullness of the Sabbath.

God's Will

Every created thing and its potential exists in order to do the will of God. That will is hidden in material nature. On Sabbath, however, the will of God is revealed.

Appreciating the Gift

God gives the Sabbath as a gift and also an elevated soul to understand the greatness of the gift.

Luck

God's gifts are received through the astrological vessels of the zodiac, their mazel. The Jewish people need to lift themselves above their mazel and receive their gifts from the root of gifts: the Sabbath.

Shade

Those who don't observe the Sabbath only see in her a lack of work, a "shadeless tree." But those who stay with her will repose and bask in her delightful shade and delicious fruit; the blessings of God.

TO DO NOTHING

During the weekdays, some do more while others do less. On the Sabbath, however, man does nothing. It is God's gift, and all receive uniformly. It unifies. And instead of individuals, we become *Klal Yisroel*, the congregation of Israel.

Three Gifts

The three gifts of wisdom, strength, and riches are offered with the Sabbath. They are real only if they are accepted with her arrival.

Word and Command

The days of the week get their life from the words God used at creation. The Sabbath, on the other hand, lives from the command of God.

A Gift

god's offer

Holiness can be earned, or received as a gift, and if not, then grabbed and taken by force. During the six workdays, we wrest from nature the spirit hidden within. But on the Sabbath, it is offered to us as a gift.

---

mortals prepare

Angels are always ready to receive, while we mortals must prepare vessels. That is the struggle and pain of earthly existence. On Sabbath, which is a gift, we receive its spirituality as a gift, too.

---

moses

Moses on Mount Sinai received 1,000 levels of holiness and understanding. When the Israelites worshiped the Golden Calf, he lost all of them except for one. Each Sabbath, however, his spiritual gifts are returned, and through him to all the Jewish people.

Male and Female

The Sabbath, as the universe, includes
both the male and female qualities.
Our great yearning for the Sabbath,
the female quality, prepares a vessel for
the gift of Sabbath, the male quality.

Holy Garments

From the intent and action of observing
the commandments, a holy garment
is woven. On the Sabbath, that garment
descends from heaven and clothes
man in its elevated soul.

Turn and Return

After God gave the Land of Israel to
Abraham, he returned it to God and then
received it as a gift. Similarly, whatever we
receive, we, too, return to God, Who gives
it to us as a gift. That is the Sabbath.

A Gift of Soul

The elevated soul we receive on the
Sabbath leaves holiness even in the
physical body of man. Thus,
his workdays are hallowed.

Double Gift

The light and holiness of the Sabbath is
on two levels. The first is a gift inside of us,
effecting the soul and inner life of each
individual. The second is a gift to the
Jewish people, an aura surrounding them,
unable to be fully received because
of its awesome holiness.

Highest Levels

Man can reach higher and higher spiritual
levels. And even levels he cannot attain on
his own, he can reach on the Sabbath.
They are purely a gift.

Covered with Light

Man can be covered with physical skin, or with light. Those are the workdays and the Sabbath.

Two Doors

There are two doors. The first leads one from the workdays to the divine realm of the Sabbath. The second door is the gateway to Sabbath itself.

Three Gifts

There are three blessings: children, health, and sustenance. On the Sabbath, when God finished, blessed and sanctified, we receive all three as a gift.

Man's Striving

All of man's striving and accomplishment does not add up to one gift of God, the Sabbath.

A Gift

The Three Perfections

On the Sabbath, we receive the three
blessings of perfection, identical to
the *kohen*-priestly blessings: protection,
grace, and peace. Together, they give us
a taste of the World to Come, unattainable
in the present state of the world.

Twins

The heavenly Sabbath waits till we are
ready, then it descends to earth. Our soul
ascends, and an elevated soul descends.
Then it is the Sabbath.

Man and Angel

God is master over those who are humble,
and Moses with his other-worldly humility
received the ultimate gift: the Sabbath.
And just as he was a man and an angel,
so, too, is the Sabbath. Half is in time,
and half is beyond.

Refuge

The Sabbath creates a house, a refuge around you, and that is its gift.

Too Perfect

The holiness of the Sabbath is too high and perfect, and there is no way we can receive it. How then do we receive it? God gives us divine vessels, the elevated soul, and with her we receive the Sabbath.

At the Door

Although the doors to the divine realm open only on the Sabbath, the Jewish people wait at the door all week long and pine to look in.

2

Infinite Light

Light

The light of the weekdays is darkness compared to the light of Sabbath. It is the original primordial light, perhaps the "flash" at the edge of the universe. And with it we can see from one end of the universe to the other; our past and our future.

Only Light

Although we may get a glimpse of light during the week, Sabbath is full of light.

The Best Perfume

The weekdays are dark compared to the
Sabbath, which is filled with light and every
good fragrance. When Sabbath ends,
we are aglow with an aroma of
the best perfumes.

To See

The light of Sabbath is concealed
within the six workdays. Thus, in the
same place, where others see
desolation, one can see light.

The Door

During the six workdays, the primeval light
of the Creation is behind closed doors. On
the Sabbath, the doors open,
and the rays shine outward.

Maturity

When the darkness is rolled away,
light is revealed in its fullness.
Thus, when Sabbath arrives, mankind is
resurrected to a complete maturity.

Moses and Aaron

Sabbath is a sign of the Creation, and a primordial light shines from a hidden place. And that same hiding place is also the safekeeping of Aaron's service and the Torah of Moses.

Full of Light

The body is darkness compared to the light of the soul. With each good deed, the body fills with bits of light. And on the Sabbath, our body and soul are equally full of light.

Hidden

In this material world, spiritual light needs to be hidden in order to be revealed. We, too, hide in our shame and receive the light of the Sabbath.

Illumination

The Sabbath light can illuminate every place and every moment of a person's life. It is his work, however, during the weekdays that makes the difference.

Darkness

During the darkness of the six workdays, man can stumble or even fall into a pit. But worse, he doesn't even know if he is on the right path. The Sabbath is a road sign, and whoever is lost can find his way.

Numbers

There is an aspect of the Sabbath that has no number; it is infinite. And there is another aspect that has number; it is the Sabbath within the workdays. By connecting the finite to the infinite, although numbered, it is without end.

Continue

From the place one had reached at the end of the Sabbath, from there he can continue to climb ever higher and continues to climb each week, without end.

Without Light

One who is surrounded by light cannot see into the darkness. But from within the darkness, we can see the light. Thus, from the weekdays, we see the light of the Sabbath. But from the Sabbath, being surrounded by light, we do not see the weekdays at all.

Total

The Sabbath is the total, complete, and absolute revelation of the inner core of holiness and purity.

Heavenly Glow

Just as when Moses descended from Mount Sinai and his face shone with a heavenly glow, so, too, do those who observe the Sabbath. Their physical skin takes on a spiritual nature.

eight

God has hidden the primordial light of Creation. It is higher than the natural world and is represented by the number eight. Prayer belongs to the natural world of seven, while Torah is from the world of eight, the World to Come. And that is the Sabbath.

A Lens

The truth is like a lens, and with it we see the truth of each creation. All truth, being pure spirit, is surrounded by falsehood. With faith, we penetrate the opacity of falsehood and see the light. Thus, with our faith during the workdays, we help bring the light of the Sabbath.

Heart

There is the heart of man and the heart of mankind. Only a sensitive heart discerns between light and darkness, the holy and the profane, redemption and exile, the six workdays and the Sabbath.

Higher Still

The Sabbath follows the six workdays.
Do they precede the Sabbath's holiness?
On some level, they are spiritually
higher, but deeply hidden.
When Sabbath arrives, the holiness
of the six days are revealed, too.

Light Itself

There are souls that are lamps,
vessels to keep the light. Others are
the light themselves. Similarly,
the six workdays are the lamps,
and the Sabbath is the light itself.

Jacob and Israel

The name *Yaakov*, Jacob, is the workdays
and their struggle to rid of evil's influence.
Yisroel, Israel, on the other hand,
is the victory over evil and the holiness
descending from heaven.
That is the Sabbath.

Lamps

There were six lamps on the menorah of the Holy Temple, each corresponding to one of the weekdays. The center of the menorah is the Sabbath, the light of the Torah given on Sabbath.

The Nations

The workdays, connected to physical acts, are accessible to all the nations. But the Sabbath, with no activity, is accessible only to the Jewish people with whom God has a covenant.

Eternal

All attributes belonging to nature, such as time, space, boundaries, and limitations are confined to the six workdays. Sabbath is infinite, timeless, eternal, and boundless.

sabbath of the sabbath

There is the Sabbath and the Sabbath of the Sabbath. In each level of the Sabbath, the top of one reaches to the bottom of the next level, so that one could strive, endlessly, for higher and higher levels of the Sabbath.

---

sabbath lamps

The light of the commandments rests on the bodily lamps, the parts of the body, and thus enlightens them. Similarly, the light of the Sabbath rests on the work of the six workdays and fills them with light.

---

stars

Each star influences some event during the weekdays. On the Sabbath, we realize that we are like the stars of the heavens. We influence them.

what's new?

In the three major holidays, we recite the *shecheyanu* blessing, thanking God to have reached that juncture in time. Sabbath's light, however, permeates all the days of the week, and therefore it is nearly not a new event.

---

holy candelabra

The Sabbath is the holy candelabra lighting up the entire year. If its petals, calyxes, and cups are added together, they equal 50, as the weeks of the year. The seven branches are the seven holy days: two of Passover, two of Succos, and one of Rosh Hashana, Yom Kippur, and Shovuos.

---

holy temple

Just as the Holy Temple spread light throughout the world, so, too, does the Sabbath.

straw

The weekdays are like straw that withers
before the glory of God, the Sabbath.

The Lamp

The soul descends only in times of
holiness, and especially on the Sabbath.
It infuses the entire man's being. It is as
a flame on a lamp, drawing all the
molecules of oil, even from the bottom.
So, too, does the Sabbath soul.
It gives vitality to every limb
and every molecule of man.

---

focus

Six years we work our field, and on the
seventh leave it fallow. Six days we work,
and the seventh day is the Sabbath.
We rest. The focus of the six is
the seventh. The six are temporary;
the seventh, permanent.

whence Light?

In the material realm, light is produced by burning away some of the material. That is the light of the workdays. The light of the Sabbath, however, is the light itself.

Looking Away

Just as we see from the "dark" part of our eye, so, too, we must look away from the darkness to see the true light. Ignore the material nature, and see only the spirit. And that is the Sabbath.

Fire

There is light that illuminates, and light that burns away. The workdays need light to burn away the chaff, while the Sabbath is illuminating light.

The Shadow

The Sabbath is the light and the weekdays are the shadow. We work all week to push away the obstacle causing the shadow and see the light directly on the Sabbath.

Man and Woman

The Hebrew word for man is *ish* and woman is *isha*, both containing the word *eish*, fire, and a yod and heh, God's name. During the workdays, in order to manifest God's name, the love of man and wife, the chaff of earthly disharmony must be consumed by fire. On the Sabbath, however, it is pure love, for no reason, and is revealed without any effort.

The Light Beyond

The six workdays must focus on the Sabbath, just as the six wicks of the menorah had to bend toward the middle lamp, because their light depended and came from the central one. Yet, even the central lamp does not have its own light. It is from the supernal light, higher than any earthly light. And that is the Sabbath.

NO LAMP

Before the Jewish people sinned, the Ten Commandments were the entire Torah and wrapped in the first words, "I am the Lord your God. . . ." That was the inner light of the Torah given on the Sabbath. Thus, Sabbath is higher than having to prepare a lamp. It is a light from the world above.

DARKNESS

No amount of darkness stands in the way of those who reveal His kingdom, the Sabbath.

GIVE CHASE

It is because you were a slave in Egypt and God redeemed you that you are able to give chase to the darkness of slavery and reveal the Sabbath.

Liberation

The six days of Creation are full of
boundaries and limitations. They are exile.
Sabbath, on the other hand, is infinite
and free from the chains of exile.
It is total liberation.

3

Holiness

Three Intervals

Friday nights, the weekdays and the Sabbath greet each other. The mundane and the holy meet. Sabbath mornings, we raise the physical aspect of the six workdays to the spiritual level of the Sabbath. And in the late Sabbath afternoons, we yearn to take along the holiness of the Sabbath into the coming week.

The Ladder

Man is a ladder, and in him the good and evil rise and descend. But the soul remains, forever, in its holiness. Sabbath is the soul of the six workdays.

Up and Down

A higher level of soul descends on the Sabbath accompanied by two angels. The soul and the angels of the weekdays ascend. Then at the end of the Sabbath, the opposite movement occurs.

The Reception

When the queen arrives, she appears to each one according to their prepared reception. So, too, is the Sabbath.

One More Drop

Just as fish, although surrounded by water, jump up for a fresh drop of rain, so, too, our souls, although surrounded by the Sabbath, jump for another drop of holiness.

Infinite Holiness

The Holy Temple in Jerusalem was a house, bounded by walls. Yet, its holiness was beyond all limits. The Sabbath is a day, yet its holiness is infinite.

pure and holy

The six workdays can be made pure; the Sabbath is holy from the start.

The commands

The six workdays were also created with God's command. Why then is the Sabbath more holy? The commands of the six days were translated into physical forms, while the Sabbath remained in its spiritual purity.

---

once

The holiness that we attain during the week is with us always. The special holiness that we receive on the Sabbath descends but once a week.

---

pioneers

Even if one can rise higher than the pioneers, they are higher by virtue of their originality and trailblazing. Similarly, although the Sabbath is holier, still, it is brought about by our pioneering effort to uncover its holiness during the workdays.

worth more

It's more worthy to God that man transforms the workdays with spirituality than the status of his soul on the Sabbath.

---

clean garments

One needs to don clean garments for the honor of the Sabbath. The body, the garment of the soul, needs to be pure in order to receive Sabbath's holiness.

---

three wonders

There are three firsts: the Creation, the Exodus, and the giving of the Torah on Mount Sinai. All three are part of the Sabbath. It is the witness to the Creation; it is a reminder of the Exodus; and the Torah was given on the Sabbath.

Direct

During the six workdays, holiness is passed down from heaven through something physical. The Sabbath, however, is given directly.

to feel the holy

The holiness of Sabbath is promised in scripture and is real enough to experience. And even those who do not feel it can believe that they have it. And they will feel it in proportion to their level of faith.

---

inner core

The universe was created with ten commands, whose inner core is the Ten Commandments. The commands are the six days of Creation, and their core is the Sabbath.

---

peeled

Just as the darkness is rolled away from before the light, so too, the dark material shells on all beings is peeled off with the arrival of the Sabbath.

The Essence

Sabbath reminds us of the Creation and
of the Exodus. The highest reminder,
however, is the most basic: Sabbath is
a holy day and brings holiness into the
world. At the onset of Sabbath, we feel
its symbol of creation; by morning,
we feel its quality of liberation; and by
the afternoon, we finally return to
its purest message. Behold!
It has brought holiness to the world.

The Depths

There is the density of the physical world,
on the one hand, and the depth of the
spiritual world, on the other hand.
By overcoming one,
we enter into the other.

Forgiveness

Just as Yom Kippur forgives
repentant sinners, so too,
the Sabbath cleans and purifies.

Even Greater

By observing the Sabbath, the Jewish people make the holiness of the Sabbath even greater.

In the Bones

Not only do we receive the holiness of the Sabbath, it goes into our bones and every part of our body.

Top to Bottom

Man is involved in two movements. He has to raise that which is on the bottom toward the heaven; and that which is on top, in heaven, he needs to bring down to the earth. When he prepares pure vessels, he receives the holiness of the Sabbath.

Ultimate Humility

A man who humbles himself to the very earth is definitely forgiven for his sins. Yet, one who does not repent with every fiber of his being is simply incapable of that kind of humility. But come the Sabbath, when all the universe humbles itself to the Creator, man can join and do the same. It is, therefore, the key to repentance.

Use Your Head

There is the head, the body, and the feet; the brain, the heart, and the liver; the soul, the spirit, and breath. We need to focus and direct our energies toward our highest level, rather than the lowest. Similarly, all our striving and focus should be the Sabbath.

Holiness Enters

Each commandment in the Torah is the spiritual twin to one of the body organs. By negating the physical life of the organ to the commandment, the light of the mitzvah enters and enlivens it. The Sabbath, too, is the spiritual twin of the weekdays. By negating the workday to the Sabbath, it receives its light.

Non-Doing

Action is physical and prevails during the six workdays. The Sabbath is the word of God, which gives life to all action. Thus by the active pursuit of Sabbath's non-doing, we infuse the workdays' doing with the holiness of non-doing.

The Whole

The observance of each of the Torah's commandments clothes a particular part of the body in holiness. Sabbath, on the other hand, clothes the entire body and soul in holiness.

without Limit

God Himself makes us holy during the Sabbath; therefore, it is without limit.

---

symbols

The commandments are the symbolic form for the spirit and holiness within the Torah. Similarly, Sabbath symbolizes the holiness descending to all creatures.

---

guards

Just as the sand guards the sea, the Jewish people guard the presence of holiness in the world. And in the measure that one struggles with the mundane to sift, refine, and separate the admixture of holiness and unholiness, so will he have it. And he who works thus during the weekdays will have the holiness of the Sabbath.

The Harp

The harp in the Temple had seven strings, just as there are seven paths to connect to the Torah. Each day of the week is another one of those paths; a new song by the Levites. The Sabbath is the focus of the days and is the harp of ten strings, found only in heaven.

The Collective

Holiness was given to the collective soul of the Jewish people forever and ever. Yet, their sins create a separation between them and God, which can be removed with repentance. On the Sabbath, when all return to be part of the collective, there is only the eternal holiness.

The King's Honor

A king shares royalty to magnify his honor. Similarly, God shares His holiness with the Jewish people. The holiness of the Sabbath, too, must be kept for God's sake.

when

When holiness is revealed, the evil forces go into hiding; when holiness is victorious, Amalek, the nemesis of the Jewish nation, is defeated. When the Sabbath arrives, all work ceases, and the memory of the workdays fades into oblivion.

---

all Dimensions

When a new light descends from above, that is holiness. The place: the Holy Temple; the time: the Sabbath; and the being: the soul within the head.

The Edge of the Sea

The Jewish people are as the sand at the edge of the sea. They protect it and gather to protect the world from a flood of incest. Thus, they reveal the ever presence of holiness, and it is the Sabbath.

Gathering

Individuals gather to form the group, and all the moments and days gather to form the Sabbath.

The Means

Although a father and mother are partners with God in forming a child, obviously, the entire process is in God's hands. The parents are merely the means. Similarly, the Sabbath is the means by which man receives holiness from heaven.

Life with Spirit

There are three partners in man: God, Who contributes the spirit, father, and mother, through whom the body is formed. Similarly, the six weekdays are of material nature. Sabbath is the spirit within the Creation. Therefore, if one is directed by his parent to desecrate the Sabbath, it is as if he is asked to give up his spirit for his body!

separated

Just as God is totally and completely separated from the world, so too, the Jewish people are separated from the nations. But of course, this is impossible to attain. On the Sabbath, however, they can accomplish it.

---

sabbath descends

The holiness of the Sabbath descends to the Jewish people to whatever level they are at present.

---

to see

Man ought to connect his material activity to its spiritual roots. He then would "see" the spirit in all that he looks at. Similarly, the Sabbath is the spiritual root of the weekdays, and one is able to see the Sabbath in each of them.

More Holy?

How can man make the Sabbath holy?
It is already as holy as it will ever be!
By drawing the holiness of the Sabbath
into the workdays, the holiness
itself intensifies.

First

First, man must take care not to
profane and cheapen the
Sabbath; then, he can make it holy.

Too Holy

Sabbath is too holy for it to be revealed
in this world. It takes the faithful,
Jewish people to reveal it.
Thus, the fact of Sabbath is also
witness to their faithful observance.

In the Depths

The Sabbath is in the deepest depth of one's heart. It is the princess from the king's palace visiting us in our home. The holidays, on the other hand, are national festivals, manifestly celebrated, and the people must leave their homes and journey to the Holy Temple.
A separation must be made.

Energy

Man's soul in his body is compared to God's presence in the universe. The soul, however, is merely a lamp, a vessel receiving God's vitality. During the six workdays, man energizes his soul by means of observing the commandments. On the Sabbath, it receives energy straight from God.

4

Spiritual Warmth

The Form

The six workdays are like wax,
obscuring the form beneath.
Sabbath is a flame that melts the wax and
reveals the form; and it is divine.

Fire

The passion and yearning to unite with
the Creator, to cast away every earthly
desire, cease all activity, and rely
solely on God, that is the Sabbath.

Two Paths

Each day has a corresponding spiritual day
on high. There are then two paths:
Raise each day to its spiritual level,
or connect it to the Sabbath.

Fragrant Garments

The Sabbath is woven from the threads of
man's good deeds in the six workdays.
They also become the garments of his
soul. And their fragrance comes from the
Garden of Eden and the World to Come.

Wisdom

Two people can do the identical act.
The wise one connects to the inner core,
while the fool experiences merely the shell.
This is the foolishness of the workdays
and the wisdom of the Sabbath.

Spiritual Warmth

Nourishment

We need to eat the Sabbath, ingest it,
so that it flows through our body
and nourishes every part of our life.

Cannot wait

We cannot wait for the arrival of the
Sabbath and, therefore, start it a few
moments earlier while it is still Friday.

Masters and slaves

The six workdays are ruled by the laws
of nature wherein some are masters and
some are slaves. Thus, the root of slavery
is from the six, while redemption
is from the Sabbath.

Safe

Sabbath is the hiding place,
the safekeeping for all blessings.
All who wish to enjoy God's
providence must connect to the Sabbath.

Fire

The natural fire of the six workdays
consumes. The fire of the Sabbath makes
one glow with spiritual delight.

All Time

Just as there is a place encompassing all
places, and it is the Holy Temple, there is
also a time that encompass all time,
and it is the Sabbath.

In and Out

God's light and holiness is revealed
and concealed in a never ending cycle.
The holiness of the Sabbath waits in the
distance during the weekdays. Those who
have longing eyes see it from afar.

Thoughts

Sabbath is so lofty that one ought not
even have thoughts of work.

Spiritual Warmth

yearning

From whence the yearning in man's heart for spiritual heights? It is from the soul, which has given him a taste of the spirit. Now he seeks to find it. The Sabbath, too, fills man with a holiness for которой he yearns and looks for all week long.

---

collective

There are the individual days, and there is the collective of all the days, and that is the Sabbath. The Sabbath is the root of all the days.

Nurturing

Sabbath is the spiritual nurturing of all faithful. And before a child is initiated as a member of the Jewish nation with circumcision, he must live through one Sabbath. Therefore, the Jewish people received the Sabbath before the holidays.

True Love

We recognize God's love for the world by delving and seeing the infinite care with which He made each and every creature. We realize His love, and our heart fills with love for Him, too. The truth of God's love, however, is beyond the Creation, beyond reason or proof. It just is. And one who returns this love has connected to the truth of the universe. And that is the Sabbath.

Many Waters

The Sabbath is the fire of love, and the weekdays are the many waters capable of extinguishing the fire. And in the end, love conquers.

All Is Good

The universe in its collective nature is very good, although it is not always united to receive the blessing. But just as the Sabbath is about to start, at twilight, there is a great rush, and all unite with the One.

The Brook

God planted a brook of fresh water,
the essence of the Torah in every Jewish
heart. On the Sabbath, the impediments
are removed, and the water flows to
every part of the body.

Presence

One ought to remember every instant
that he is in God's presence. Of course,
during the workdays, this is impossible.
On the Sabbath, though,
we nearly achieve it.

Parting with Friends

It is hard to part with a good friend.
And man, too, longs not to forget the
taste of the Sabbath when it leaves.
And at its inception, knowing that it
will soon be over, he is careful not
to miss one instant of it.

Master

Man has to allow the part of his soul called man to know God, and that soul to be master over his animal self and then to serve God with deeds. Similarly, the workdays are to repair the animal self, and the Sabbath lifts the soul to celestial heights.

Return Again

Each divine spark in concealment is in prison and guarded by evil. It is our task to set free, to reveal those holy sparks no matter what vessel they are in now. Then we must return that spark to its roots, in God. This is our work of the six workdays, followed by the Sabbath when we return our finds to the Creator.

5

In God's Presence

The Root

Sabbath is the root of the Creation, the inner core and truth of each being. Each day further from the Sabbath is further from the truth. Thus, the first three days of the week move away from Sabbath, while the next three days move toward her.

The King's Seal

Everything that is royalty has the king's seal. Sabbath is that seal. During the week, we do not recognize the world as royal property. On Sabbath, however, it becomes crystal clear.

The Source

We are not perfect, nor will we ever be.
Everything has some chaff. Still, all yearn
for perfection, to return to the source.
When Sabbath arrives, all return to the
source, and all chaff falls away.

Sabbath Is in All

Each creation contains its matter;
its creator; its creative act; and its purpose.
The Creator's purpose, coupled with
the act of creating, is the Sabbath,
and thus each contains the Sabbath.

Life Itself

Cut off from their roots, the days of the
week are dead. They have life only from
the Sabbath. Thus, those who observe
the Sabbath give life to the entire week.

vanity

How can a declaration of God's kingdom
be significant? Does He need us?
Yes, all mankind needs us to negate the
preponderance of vanity in the world,
and, especially on the Sabbath, to negate
all physical power and importance
of the six workdays.

---

ego

Sabbath is the day when all creatures let
go of their egos, power, and arrogance.
Instead, they concede that God is He
Who gives the energy for all action.

---

birth

Birth and renewal need great protection.
Therefore, God covers and protects with
His "wings" all who observe the Sabbath.

The Light

Although darkness prevails, our faith in God's light is unshakable. And while the forces of darkness prevail and use up all their evil, God guards the light for his faithful. Similarly, the light of the Sabbath is guarded and available for those who long for it.

Exposed

That which is always covered needs protection when uncovered; as the brain, heart, or liver during surgery. Similarly, our inner hearts are exposed during the Sabbath and need much protection.

Gates

Sabbath is the main gate to God's palace. Through her portal, one enters to commune with God, and it is always open. And through it, the immortal soul sees eternally into the future.

Faith and Truth

There is faith, "Thus spoke the Lord," in the six workdays and truth on the Sabbath. "This is the word of God."

Like Angels

It is no surprise that we observe the Torah when we are like people, during the six workdays. But on the Sabbath, too, when we are like angels, in the presence of the infinite, we still do as we were commanded.

Like Father, Like Son

A prince does not have to learn royal conduct; after all, he is a son of his father. How else would he behave? A servant, on the other hand, must overcome his nature in order to please his master, the king. Similarly, we are in the palace as sons of the king on the Sabbath.

seeds

A farmer plants a seed and leaves it in the ground. He surrenders his action and lets God take over. On the Sabbath, too, man surrenders all his activity to God.

---

tent

Man can build the strongest house, yet be washed away by flood. It had no foundation in God. Another can pitch a tent, completely relying on God, and it will stand forever. That is the Sabbath.

---

protection

Because the Jewish people live in the realms above the laws of nature, they need great divine protection. And that is the Sabbath.

Home

A physical being needs a place and a time. On the Sabbath, God provides His space and time for all who come home to Him. And for all those who have neither a place nor time, suddenly they are home.

Love and Awe

There is the awe and the love of God. In exile, we start with awe, and it brings love. In the land of Israel, we start with the love of God, and that brings us to the awe of Him. Similarly, during the six workdays, we start with awe, while on the Sabbath we start with the love of God.

Servants

A servant is always at the whim of his master and is therefore always praying. A son, on the other hand, wherever he may be, is the son of his father and is able to search the treasury, the Torah. On the Sabbath, we are welcomed as children of God and find Him in every move.

Blessing

Sabbath is the root of all blessings
before they even start to filter into
the physical world.

Speaking

God spoke to us face to face with Ten
Commandments, and those words are
still being said to us. Thus, we consecrate
our speaking to each other on the Sabbath
and the topics of discussion.

Freedom

The natural world is a "house of slaves": all
who are bound by her limitations. During
the Sabbath, we can find freedom by
connecting with the Creator's plan.

Battle

The weekdays are a time of war,
a battle necessary to elevate the soul's
spirituality. Finally, on the Sabbath,
it basks in God's warmth.

The Cracks

All week long we feel God's watchfulness
through cracks in the walls between
Him and us. On the Sabbath,
the walls are removed.

Rising

The spirit on the Sabbath soars higher and
higher. And when our physical self does
not hinder the soul from rising, it, too,
rises from its level.

Three Levels

There are three levels to the Sabbath.
The first is connected to physical vitality.
Man needs to observe, to refrain from
producing physical changes of
consequence on the Sabbath. The second
is connected to the spirit, to sanctify the
day with a declaration. And the third
is the highest and is the elevated soul
that descends on the Sabbath.

to forget

When we enter the World to Come in the afterlife, we forget the material world completely. Sabbath, too, to a lesser degree, is like that. We forget the toil and suffering of the world.

---

children

As servants of God during the workdays, we feel inadequate to receive the holiness of the Sabbath. And with that humility, we are drawn close to God and rise to the level of children.

---

righteous

The righteous who cleave to God, all their days are like the Sabbath.

---

in essence

The essence of the Sabbath is that God is the Creator and sustains the universe every instant.

NO TIME

If one has no place, God gives him a place. And if one has no time, God gives him time. And that is the Sabbath.

LEVEL OF SABBATH

One who negates all his work and deeds of the weekdays to the Sabbath is transformed to the level of the Sabbath.

ALWAYS THERE

How can the holiness of the Sabbath be confined to a particular day? Isn't it beyond time? It is from the world beyond time and is there always. On Sabbath, though, God allows us to discern its holiness.

JOY IN JOY

One whose heart is empty of himself, and instead is full of the joy of God with His Creation, is about to be filled with blessing.

choosing

God's kingdom is hidden, allowing man to
be independent and free to choose.
As soon as man learns the inside story,
of God's providence and kingdom, he
realizes that He and He alone is king
and ruler. Then the more he delves,
the more he understands.
And that is the Sabbath.

---

we respond

When God meets us face to face, talks to
us, and we respond, would it not be
embarrassing if He spoke and we ignored
Him? But that shame and humility would
make us worthy, in a small measure,
to meet Him face to face.
And that is the Sabbath.

---

in our heart

When we connect to the Sabbath with all
our heart, its holiness remains in there.
And wherever we go throughout the week,
the Sabbath is there with us.

A place

No one has a place in the world unless granted by God. The Sabbath is that place. It is the very base of the foundation just as the *Even Sh'tiah*, the stone in the Holy of Holies, of the Holy Temple, from whence the earth spread.

In god's presence

The first instant of Creation, the world was still in God's presence, without intermediaries. Then as it spread, it was dominated by natural laws. On the Sabbath, it all returned to God's presence.

The cause

What could man do or accomplish in God's presence? There, all is null and void. He is the cause of all causes, and we are merely the effect. The Sabbath lifts all our efforts to God, and the effects become the cause.

A place

The righteous have their place in the Sabbath, while the repentants yearn all week long for it. And, with their yearning create their own place in the Sabbath.

The Brook

Downstream, there is danger and hiddenness. But at the source of the brook, all is quiet and full of life.
And that is the Sabbath.

Standing before God

When a creature is face to face with God, it is at the root of providence. It is the place of all gifts. Is man prepared to receive it? Only on the Sabbath when all creatures reach out for perfection, then they are well prepared to receive.

Angels

During the week, we are merely men; but on the Sabbath, we are angels standing before God.

who comes?

The Jewish people don't wait for the
Sabbath to come to them.
They come to the Sabbath.

---

only His

All life and energy are from God, and
all work and accomplishment are His.
It was His and it is His, which is what
we feel on the Sabbath. And if not,
is there greater shame?

The Afterlife

All the preparations of the week are for
the Sabbath. Similarly, the work of this life
is for the afterlife, the World to Come.

---

without garments

Just as Adam stood without garments
before God, so, too, the Sabbath needs
no intermediary and stands on its
own before God.

Free

One who is free of the evil urge is
already in the World to Come.
That is the Sabbath.

The Moment

The weekdays are composed of seconds,
minutes, and hours. The Sabbath is the
moment, a moment that presents
itself as the absolute present.

Beckoning

The Sabbath day itself beckons to the
soul of man to praise God. And those
who are worthy hear her call.

Transform

The purpose is to tie the Sabbath to the six
workdays, thereby transforming them.

In God's Presence

Make Room

As the sun sets and Sabbath begins,
the created makes way for the uncreated.
Work makes room for rest, and bread
steps aside for the mana, the bread
of heaven.

True Desire

Man's true desire can be in exile.
On the Sabbath, it is free.

Troops

Just as a sovereign gives food for his
troops, so, too, does God to those who
proclaim His kingdom. On the Sabbath,
those who do but God's bidding are fed
with His pleasure and sustenance.

Honor of Kings

One honors God with concealment, while
kings are honored by revealing their deeds.
The six days of Creation are the acts of
God: concealed. The seventh day,
Sabbath, declares His kingdom!

Appearances

The Sabbath is the root of all blessing, and the Jewish people are its vessel. This is true merely in the most sublime and secret way. But superficially, the Sabbath seems barren of work and accomplishment, and the Jewish people seem the lowliest and empty of all earthly power.

Health

All health and sickness comes from eating. On the Sabbath, eating is a mitzvah, as part of respecting the Sabbath, and brings good health.

The Temple

The holiness of the Sabbath is among the Jewish people and is indestructible. And even if the Holy Temple was destroyed, its holiness is still with us during the Sabbath.

In God's Presence

Lifting the Head

One must lift his head and live on a higher
plane. When "rosh," head, is lifted to the
next letter the reish is shin, aleph is beis,
and shin is tav, and it spells Shabbos,
the Sabbath. If we lift our heads,
we are living with the Sabbath.

Roots

One must always yearn not to be
separated from the root of his soul in the
one and only God. And that is the Sabbath
and repentance, returning to the roots.

Don't Know

The more spiritually enlightened one is
the more he knows that he doesn't know.
And on the Sabbath, when one
receives two crowns of wisdom,
he realizes it the most.

cleaned

One may repent, but a residue of sin
remains. By observing the Sabbath,
even that thin film is cleaned
from him until pure.

---

among evil

During the weekdays, man works among
both the good and the evil. On the
Sabbath, whose purity and holiness knows
no bounds, some of the evil is erased.

---

one half

Each creation is one half of a whole.
There is the celestial fire and the earthly
fire; the Torah that descends from heaven
and the one that returns from the earth.
Thus, although we have our soul, the soul
of the soul descends on the Sabbath.

gates

Each Sabbath, another gate of the fifty gates of understanding opens. And he who is worthy gets to enter all of them in a year's cycle.

---

start again

On their own, created beings get old. In the presence of God, however, they find renewal. There, at the root of all being, they are able to start again.

---

love calls

The Sabbath itself lovingly calls to each one of us to come, cleave, and be enlightened in God's presence.

---

pleasure

The Garden of Eden consisted of three spiritual entities: Eden (delight), *nahar* (stream), and *Gan* (the Garden), in acrostic, *o-n-e-g,* pleasure. Spelled backward, it is *n-e-g-a*, a leprous curse. Those who find pleasure in the Sabbath also find their spiritual counterparts.

Rough and smooth

The path toward evil seems smooth to start but later turns rough. The path of God is at first rough; one must begin with hard work, then he receives the gift of enlightenment. It is also true that the more one seeks the light in the six workdays, the greater his light of Sabbath will be.

Longing

Man ought to be longing always to be in God's presence, which is his origin and end. That is the longing for the Sabbath.

Separate

When the Jewish people separate from the nations to achieve their goals, they are then able. And when they pursue their goals, they are able to separate from the nations. Similarly, when we connect to the Sabbath, holiness is revealed, and the darkness of the workdays vanishes.

Mana

Although the mana, the heavenly bread, did not descend on the Sabbath, it is the root of the mana and the blessings of the entire week.

God's Name

God sealed His name into every single Jew, and He also sealed His name into the Sabbath. One must not desecrate God's name, which is in him, nor the name in the Sabbath.

Holy Work

The types of work done in the Holy Tabernacle are the very ones forbidden to be done on the Sabbath. There, the holiness was within the work; on the Sabbath, it is revealed.

opposites

The heavenly realm is the opposite of the material realm. They are at odds and are perpetually in dynamic opposition. On the Sabbath, however, both are present, in peace and tranquility.

The Link

Sabbath is the link between the physical and the spiritual worlds. It is, therefore, a covenant, that which links the two partners.

Work

To have the Sabbath, we must work during the six workdays. And with its arrival, we hide our common work in favor of the divine, spiritual light descending.

Our Lamp

God lights our lamp, our soul, during the workdays; and He is our lamp on the Sabbath.

Negating

By negating our will to God's will,
we can discern between the good
and evil of the workdays.

Life and Death

Life seems light and death, like darkness,
seems dark. But the truth is, that in the
midst of darkness there is light;
where it seems most difficult,
the most light is hidden.

Two Brothers

The two brothers Moses and Aaron,
one with the Torah, the other with
protection of peace, constantly sustain
the Jewish people. And when the people
unite as one, as on the Sabbath,
they receive gifts from them.

Animals

We are either the children of God or His servants. And even if we are as low as an animal, that creature also has to rest on the Sabbath. But one who accepts the Sabbath on the lowest level, as an animal, merits to observe it on the next higher level until the highest as children.

Body Rest

The least we must do on the Sabbath is to rest our body from the hard work of the workdays. Then, we invite the elevated soul to enter us.

Hand and Head

The *tefilin* of the hand represents the body, and the *tefilin* of the head represents the Torah. We never wear the head's *tefilin* without the hand's. Similarly, we should first observe the Sabbath, bodily rest, then remember the Sabbath with Torah.

in the vestibule

We are in the vestibule of the palace preparing to meet the king. By observing the commandments, we create a lamp for God's light. When the divine nature of all the parts of our body is revealed, it shines with divine light. And this is even more true on the Sabbath.

6

The Torah

speaking

All week long, as servants, we speak to Him through prayer. But on the Sabbath, as children of God, He speaks to us through the Torah.

The Truth

On the Sabbath, the Jewish people are able to tell the truth: that God created the world. It is, therefore, a day of truth, and the truth of the Torah is also revealed.

The Test

Those who are connected to the Tree
of Knowledge, an admixture of good
and evil, constantly need God's help.
Challenged, they stumble. But the Sabbath
is the Tree of Life, and with it
the test can be overcome.

To Listen

"All that God had spoken, we will do
and we will listen." "We will do"
are the six workdays, and
"we will listen" is the Sabbath.

Torah

The Torah was given on the Sabbath.
Therefore, the Jewish people are able
to abandon all work on that day and,
in quietude, listen to the word of God.

The Torah

Truth

When truth is revealed, all righteous are redeemed, and the wicked cower. Similarly, the truth of the Sabbath brings redemption.

To See and to Know

Some people need to see the truth, others know it. Before the Torah was given, they saw that the mana rested on the seventh day. After, they knew that the Sabbath is God's day of rest.

Sabbath's Torah

The Torah must be brought into man's everyday lest it waste away. On the Sabbath, however, even if nothing needs doing, still the Torah remains.

Torah Revealed

The Torah is read on the Sabbath to show that it is revealed on this holy day.

without garments

The oral Torah law, the details of all action, is our guide for the workdays. The written Torah, without garments, is our guide for the Sabbath.

Three Days

Just as there were three days of preparation, at Mount Sinai, before receiving the Torah on the Sabbath, so, too, there are before each Sabbath.

Fifty-Three Portions

The Torah is divided into fifty-three portions, one for each Sabbath of the year. Still, the entire Torah are God's names in different combinations. Therefore, the Torah that appears to us is a mirror image of the Torah we have prepared during the workdays.

house of slaves

Our souls have two levels. During the six workdays, our soul is from the "house of slaves." On the Sabbath, however, it is from the level of Mount Sinai, the world of freedom.

---

witnesses

How can the Jewish people be witnesses for the Creation of so long ago? They recollect by reading the contract that they had signed: the Torah. Thus, the Torah is witness for the Sabbath.

The whole

Each of the 613 commandments in the Torah refreshes a specific part of the human body. And the Sabbath, whose caliber equals the 613 commandments, restores and revitalizes every part of the body.

only Torah

Even if during the workdays we are admonished to both labor and study the Torah, on the Sabbath we ought to dwell on Torah, exclusively.

---

mouth to mouth

The Ten Commandments, before our sin of worshiping the Golden Calf, was like a mother feeding her baby from the food in her mouth: mouth to mouth, directly receiving wisdom from God. On the Sabbath, we can feel that, again.

---

eternity

Prayer is for the here and now, the physical, temporary well-being of the person. Torah is eternal and prepares one for eternity. Similarly, the holidays enlighten the season, but the Sabbath is permanent and eternal.

The Torah

Infinite Light

There are two levels of Torah. There are the letters, words, and commandments of the Torah. They are in physical form. And there is also the light of the Torah, infinite, out of boundaries. And that is the Sabbath.

Empty Desert

One who is like a desert, empty of any substance, is a vessel to receive the Torah. The Sabbath is the day to empty all physical striving and dominion over the world. It is the ultimate preparation to receive the gift of Torah.

Beginning and End

The Jewish people are connected to the Torah prior to Creation. The end desired result is connected to the beginning intention. Sabbath, too, is connected to God's desire to create the world.

we are the torah

The twenty-two letters of the Torah
are etched into every Jewish heart.
They possess a powerful light that is
revealed through Torah study. By bearing
witness to the Creation on the Sabbath,
we become part of the Torah verses
describing the Creation, and the light
of the letters is revealed.

---

who we are

The Torah and its commandments define
who we are and why we were created.
One who forgets that is at great risk.
And so, on the Sabbath, we remember
the purpose of the Creation and are
filled with enthusiasm.

---

the torah of sabbath

The more Torah in a man's heart,
the bigger vessel he is for the Sabbath.
The more he receives the Sabbath,
the more Torah he can contain.

place and time

Everyone has his own place and time.
He who observes the Torah of Moses,
has his place in the world; and he who
adheres to Aaron's peaceful ways has
all the time in the world. Both of these
qualities converge in the Sabbath:
the place you are standing is holy,
and the time at hand is eternal.

---

at sinai

At Mount Sinai, when the Jewish people
stood face to face with the Creator,
all bodily concealment was removed.
And they knew clearly that God
created the world in 6 days
and rested on the Sabbath.

---

from above

When the Jewish people stood at Mount
Sinai, God lifted them over the heavens
and asked them to look down and see
Him creating the universe. Thus,
they are witnesses for the Sabbath.

To Join

The wisdom in the Jewish people is the Torah. Those who negate their being to the collective soul join in their wisdom and witness the Sabbath as a day of God's rest.

Prophets

The Jewish people are witnesses to the Creation, although they do not see it. And the Sabbath is also a witness that the Jewish people are prophets and sons and daughters of prophets.

Remember and Observe

The first two commandments, "I am your God . . ." and "Do not have other gods . . . ," correspond to the dual commandments, ". . . remember" and ". . . observe . . ." the Sabbath. Remember that you have no other god, and observe and keep all idol worship away from you.

six gates

Two eyes, two nostrils, two ears are the six workdays. They are gates open to receive. Sabbath is the mouth, without a pair and ready to speak words of Torah and give blessings to the world.

7

Divine Rest

Resting place

God is the resting place of all beings.
Compared to Him, everything is out
of place. In the six days of Creation,
everything moved away from God.
On the Sabbath, everything returned.
There was stillness and quiet.
They all came to rest.

Banished

During the weekdays, evil lurks behind
every good deed. On the Sabbath,
all evil is banished and has no place,
and good deeds can be
done without peril.

To Taste the Divine

One can taste the divine on the Sabbath, but first he must leave behind the limited tastes of the material world.

Finished

Man must toil during the six workdays, and his work seems never to be finished. As soon as the Sabbath arrives, a completeness and wholeness descends to the world. And no matter what man was doing, suddenly, it is complete.

Root of Creation

"In the beginning God created the heavens and the earth . . ." (Genesis 1:1). That refers not to the actual Creation, but to the root of Creation from whence all came forth. And that is God's freewilled desire: the Sabbath. Compared to the unity at the root of Creation, the Creation itself is nothing but chaos. Therefore, after the chaos of the six days of Creation, our six workdays, we return to the roots and experience complete unity and rest.

without effort

At home in its resting place, the soul does not work hard. Everything is easily accomplished without effort. That place is the Sabbath, where there are not things to do, but one.

The "wings" of God

Sabbath is the refuge for the tired, weak, and despairing. It is, so to speak, the wings of God, which shelter all who surrender themselves to its protection.

---

completion

As the sun set on the afternoon of the sixth day of Creation, some creatures never got finished. Thus, the weekdays are an incomplete vessel, like a vessel with a hole that cannot contain. Sabbath arrived and completed all missing parts.

Return

The Jewish people give back the entire Creation to God on the Sabbath. And they will not rest; they will investigate all evidence and hear all witnesses till they determine without doubt that God created the universe. That happens each week on the Sabbath.

Bribes

One ought not be enamored with bodily lusts. Those are bribery to his senses and don't allow him to see the truth.

Struggle

Man struggles with the seduction and distractions of the six workdays. God rewards him with the Sabbath, a place where no work is necessary, but to rest in His presence.

Danger

The world of nature works with immutable
laws and is, therefore, always in grave
danger. Infringements of laws have serious
consequences. Then comes the Sabbath
of total loving kindness and saves
the world.

Time

To do work, one needs time. On Sabbath,
God did no work, and neither do we. It has
no time, but is the root of all time.

Tzitzis/Fringes

Three of the strings of the *tzitzis*
are doubled to make six. Those are the
six workdays. One-half of the fourth string
is blue and wound around the others.
The other half of it is white.
That corresponds to the Sabbath.
It is half in heaven and half on earth.

for its own sake

It is true that the Sabbath infuses the entire week with its holiness. Still, they are merely six days. Its observance needs to be infinite, for its own sake.

---

rest

The path to holiness is composed of two parts: ceasing from all evil and doing good. Sabbath, too, has the negative and positive aspects: to come to a complete rest and to rest.

---

to feel

The Sabbath is a blessing, and slavery is a curse. If one is enslaved by the attachments of the workdays, he cannot feel the blessing of the Sabbath.

---

sifting

To work, sift through, and find the holy sparks in exile and exiled souls is the task of the six workdays. The Sabbath, however, is exclusively given to the Jewish people. It is their redemption.

Before and After

When we observe the Sabbath after an entire week of work, we realize that our success was caused by God. Then, it can be followed by another week of work.

Orderly

The six workdays are orderly and bound within limitation. They have sequence, passing with a rhythm, evening, morning, day after day. Sabbath, on the other hand, is higher than space and time and is infinite.

Pressure

One who is pressured by his workload, is limited in time, and still drops everything to honor the Sabbath will be rewarded to live without limitations or pressure.

Friday

Friday, after the hour of noon, the light rays of the Sabbath are already filtering into the waning workdays. Those who yearn to bask in their light readily see them.

Heavenly Sabbath

There is the Sabbath that can only exist
in heaven, and there is the one on earth.
We, therefore, receive Sabbath's elevated
soul from heaven, and, with it, it is
kept on earth as it is in heaven.

Numbers

The Jewish people have the quality
of number and beyond number.
Although numbers seem to be without end,
they are of the finite world. The six
workdays are connected to number.
The Sabbath, to infinity.

Two Breads

The Sabbath is honored with two breads.
One is the bread of affliction, a week
of hard work. The other is
of the heaven, of the Sabbath.

The Battle

The powers of evil cover up and hide God's kindness. Thus, during the six workdays, man thinks that accomplishment is his doing and not God's. We must fight this tendency, and without rest declare God's providence. That is the work of the weekdays. On the Sabbath, we finally rest from our battle.

New

There is spiritual newness, and there is the illusion of the new. If one is connected to the Sabbath and its newness, then he is spared from illusion.

Without Sabbath

Till the Sabbath arrives, we cannot imagine how we will ever partake in its awesome holiness. Yet, an instant after it starts, we cannot imagine how we could ever have been without it.

Divine Nature

The divine nature of the Sabbath becomes part of those who observe it.

Speak

During the six workdays, one cannot be fully a Jew, to pray and declare God's kingdom. On the Sabbath, he is released from "prison" and is free to speak.

Hard Work

When a child is wicked, parents feel the difficulty and heaviness of their work. God, too, so to speak, has difficulty when humanity is not up to par. But on the Sabbath, even the plainest have awe of Him. And, thus, He has rest.

A Point

Lines and objects are limited. The spiritual, on the other hand, is a point, but infinite. It contains every blessing, every color, and every taste. And those who observe the Sabbath receive them all.

feast

The root of material space, of time and
of spirit, is in the Sabbath. In her,
they all feast and are able to continue.

---

infinite desire

Whatever man desires is finite.
But those who fear God negate their
desire to God's infinite desire.
On the Sabbath, we reach beyond
our limits to the infinite that
God is ready to give.

---

six at a time

The Sabbath gives vitality for the six
coming workdays. And thus, man's
involvement should be for the span
of six days. Following the next Sabbath,
he can again get involved for six days.

Lifting Up

We need to work hard during the six workdays to lift the holy sparks from their material exile. We must leave our place and seek them. On the Sabbath, we are at rest in our place, and the holy sparks come to us for redemption.

The Rose

There is a rose among the thorns, and it is the holiness of the Sabbath within the six workdays. Most see only the thorns. When the Sabbath arrives, however, the rose unfolds for the faithful.

Renewal of Renewal

The Creation is renewed; all things and creatures get a new lease on life. But even the renewal is renewed, and that is on the Sabbath.

Doing by Not Doing

How do we do the Sabbath? By not doing. By negating all our doing to the not, God's doing, we get done.

Preparing

God spoke to the Israelites twice about the Sabbath: before they sinned with the worship of the Golden Calf and afterward. Some are able to prepare for the Sabbath during the weekdays, while others need the Sabbath to prepare for the weekdays.

Time

There is earthly time and spiritual time. The Sabbath is the channel through which we are connected to spiritual time.

Happiness

The World to Come is everlasting happiness and so is the Sabbath in a small measure. Still, no individual may receive it, only the congregation of Israel. By uniting as one, they all receive it on the Sabbath.

Greatness

On Sabbath, we put to rest the notion that nature diminishes God's greatness. On the contrary, we discover His greatness, and all arrogance comes to a screeching halt.

Natural Time

The six days of Creation are called days. The Sabbath is not part of days, of natural time. It is the soul of the workdays.

Desire Alone

Although the six workdays need activity, striving, and work to accomplish, the Sabbath needs none. Desire alone is enough.

God's Rest

When created beings allow God to rule over them, He has rest. The wicked, with their rebellion, make Him "tired." The righteous, level upon endless level, struggle to reestablish His rest.

ROOT LAWS

Each human being is ruled by the laws of nature and also by the roots of those laws, their spirit in heaven. Those divine roots are given to the Jewish people with the Sabbath.

MAN'S SPEECH

With speech, man commands and rules over the Creation. But does he? He is powerless in God's presence. On the Sabbath when this is revealed, his very speech is changed and different.

ONLY GOD

Not an angel, not a *saraf*, nor a celestial messenger brings the Sabbath to mankind. Only God, His honor and singular being, brings it.

Being and Becoming

Prior to the Creation of the universe, there was the one and only God. We use the name yod-heh-vav-heh (*Havayeh*), Being and Becoming. After the first act of Creation and He was master and king, we use the name E-lo-him. Sabbath returns us to the name *Havayeh*, to God prior to the world, or people, or action.

If Not Mercy

The six workdays are connected to God as king and master, who judges and metes out judgment, measure for measure. But the world would never survive if not for mercy and loving kindness. That is the Sabbath. Although blemished with sin and undeserving, still, it is given to us.

Waiting for Sabbath

The Jewish people are known as *Shomrei Shabbos*, those who observe the Sabbath; and they really have no higher endeavor than to wait for the Sabbath, to yearn and pine for it all week long.

shame

When Sabbath arrives, we are ashamed of our meager accomplishments during the six workdays. As Sabbath ends, we still feel spiritually unaccomplished, and that completes our observance.

---

common goods

A king invited himself to his friend for dinner. With great excitement, the friend prepared the house with the best of his household: common and cheap goods. Just then, the king entered with the finery of the palace, leaving his friend in great shame. The sensitive king said, "No, I will not use mine, but only yours!" And we, will we welcome Him again with common and cheap rubbish on the Sabbath?

A Taste

Sabbath is a taste of the World to Come. And although the commandments are beyond understanding till the future, on Sabbath they are understood.

free slave

One may think that the Sabbath is divinely
lofty and beyond his reach. Therefore,
the Torah also includes the reason,
" . . . because you were a slave in Egypt
and God freed you. . . ." It is for you,
too, because you, too, were freed.

---

pleasure

The Creation is, so to speak, God's
complete pleasure and satisfaction,
and that became complete on the Sabbath.

---

two aspects

Both the physical and spiritual universe
have an inner and outer aspect and
are hidden and revealed. When one
is revealed, the other is concealed.
And on the Sabbath, we hide the
outer aspect, work, to the utmost
in order to fully reveal the inner part.

Respite

During the six workdays, there is a battle with the evil forces, and one has difficulty establishing God's kingdom. Sabbath is a respite; evil flees, and we are at rest.

Give Up

There are those who do not feel the peaceful rest of the Sabbath. Still, they give up their work and participate in the rest. And for that, they merit that they will experience true rest.

Granted

Whoever observes the Sabbath is granted the desire and yearning for the best of the spiritual.

At the End

If one works and negates all his striving to the divine spark, he finally, at the end, arrives at divine rest.

one

The work of man's life-work is to connect all the parts and produce one unity. And when all is one, the light comes to rest on the lamp. And that is the Sabbath.

---

elevated soul

The World to Come is the opposite of this material world and cannot tolerate it. Still, the Sabbath is the World to Come, and we receive it with our elevated soul.

---

reward

The fact that the Jewish people have and observe the Sabbath is a sign that they will receive the World to Come, which the Sabbath is.

---

wisdom

One ought to negate his ignorant body to the wisdom of his mind. Then he will get strength to observe the Torah even when his wisdom does not agree. That is the blessing that the Sabbath gives to the six workdays.

Riches

Riches are a mixture of joy and sadness.
If one uses the Sabbath as the vessel
in which blessings are received,
then there is only joy.

The Gates

At first, one has to accept upon himself
the yoke of heaven and then observe
the commandments. How then could
the gates of one's heart open if not
by desire and action? The desire
is the Sabbath, and the action
is the six workdays.

Soul

Every physical action has roots in the
spiritual world. Man has a soul that adds
wisdom to his actions. There is, however,
a portion of that soul that does not
combine with the body in any manner,
and that we experience on the Sabbath.

sealed

As long as desolation and confusion dominated during the six days of Creation, the divine origin of the world remained hidden. When the concealment was removed, divinity was revealed. And so it was on the Sabbath that God's name was sealed on the universe.

complete

At first, the Creation was fragmented and was many individuals. With the Sabbath, the Creation reached completeness, and a unity was formed. It was one.

8

Remembering

God's Will

Every desire in man is born of God's will.
We need to know, though, what God wills.
On the Sabbath, when we fill with
enthusiasm for God's holiness,
we know His will, too.

Two Aspects

In each of the Torah's commandments,
there is the temporary and the permanent.
By refraining from work on the Sabbath,
we humble the body and admit its
impermanence. By dwelling on the
memory of the Sabbath, which shares
the holiness of our soul, we
connect to immortality.

Body and Soul

A child's body, as well as his soul,
is connected to that of his parents.
He looks at his body and remembers them.
That is prophesy. On the spiritual level,
we are one with the spirit of God.
And that is the Sabbath.

True Visage

One does not even recognize himself
nor does he really know his own
greatness until the Sabbath arrives.

To Return

During the week, we take everything
for ourselves. On the Sabbath,
we return everything to God.

Consciousness

How are the diverse activities, styles,
and people united? It is with a singular,
tribal consciousness, all intent on serving
the Creator. That consciousness
is the Sabbath.

Jacob and Israel

Man needs to forget the vanities of this
world and to remember only the Sabbath.
The struggle with vanities is of Jacob,
and the victory is of Israel.
He overcame and came to rest.

Two Parts

There is the fear and love of God;
the planting and the reaping;
observing and remembering the Sabbath.
One is the vessel, and the other fills it up.

Nothing But

There are two aspects of the Sabbath:
to remember, to think of nothing but
the total peacefulness of the Sabbath;
the other is to observe, to carefully
refrain from all work on the Sabbath.

impermanent

On the occasions when God redeems us, we then know that our exile is but temporary. Similarly, when the Sabbath arrives, we realize that the material world of the six workdays is impermanent. And thus, we are redeemed.

---

secrets

Because wine reveals secrets, we use it in consecrating the Sabbath, revealing spiritual secrets to those who observe it.

Dangerous place

Man was sent to a world perilous to spiritual growth. All is illusion and misleading. Can he stay on track? Only by seeking the Sabbath, the holiness, and spark of divine vitality in each thing.

---

success

During the six workdays, it appears as if the wicked are succeeding. On the Sabbath, we realize that it is but an illusion. Success is for those connected to the Sabbath.

Giving

All creatures receive in order to give. They are a vessel for God's gifts and use those gifts to declare His kingdom, to receive the holiness of the Sabbath, and add to its holiness by remembering her.

Remembering

To remember is to keep the Sabbath in one's heart always, yearning for it all week, to remember it, with every new encounter: "Perhaps I ought to save this for the Sabbath."

---

wisdom

When one matures, he regards the "wisdom" of his youth as foolishness, and this can progress without end. What is one to do? He must negate himself to the root of all wisdom: God. That opportunity comes on the Sabbath.

set aside

In every act, to set aside a portion
untouched, but for God alone:
that is the Sabbath.

---

shame

The word Shabbos also spells *bo'shes*,
shame. One who removes himself from
the confusion of evil will be embarrassed
more and more about his shortcomings.
And during the workdays, he will be
ashamed that he had not reached
the level of the Sabbath.

---

all the same

Although some commandments are easy
while others are hard to observe, at their
roots they are all the same: God's
commands. During the Sabbath,
the root of the commands,
one can experience this.

The Yoke of Heaven

Those who accept the yoke of heaven
are liberated from the yoke of others.
But while in prison, how could we ever
be free? By realizing that the prison itself
is a decree of heaven. Thus, with the
liberation of the Sabbath, we can accept
the yoke of heaven. And by waiting
for the Sabbath, we realize that
the yoke of the six workdays is
from heaven, too.

The Nest

After flying around the six workdays,
the bird finally finds its nest and rests.
That is the Sabbath.

Faith and Truth

To the degree that one lives with faith
during the six workdays, he receives
the truth of the Sabbath.

foundations

In God's restful satisfaction with the
Creation on the Sabbath lie the two
foundations of our faith: that God created
the world ex nihilo, from nothing;
and that we have total freedom
to choose His kingdom.

---

wisdom

The root of wisdom and the highest
wisdom is to know God. It is hidden
during the week and revealed
on the Sabbath.

---

the voice

The voice of God is His energy within
His word. His word is hidden within
the Creation and may be forgotten.
It, therefore, needs protection.
To *observe* the Sabbath is to protect
the word; to *remember* the Sabbath
is to hear the voice, which needs
no protection.

only

If we set aside the six workdays for all of
our work and the seventh day only for rest,
then our work will surely get done.

---

forgetting

When the soul is sent to the physical
world, it forgets the great celestial light.
On the Sabbath, it is bathed in
that light again.

---

work

The greatest and truest good hidden within
nature is received as a gift from God.
Only those who work for it receive it.
Similarly, Sabbath is always there,
but only those who prepare receive
all her blessings.

Beliefs

A Jew needs to believe in three things: God created the universe; He governs it; and the world will be fully redeemed and God's kingdom established. The Sabbath is witness to each of the three: the Creation; the giving of the Law; and that one day Sabbath peace will descend, never to leave.

Three spheres

During the Sabbath, we rise through the three spheres. We observe the Sabbath by resting from all work: with action. We receive the Sabbath by studying its Torah laws: with speech. And we arrive at the pinnacle of holiness by enjoying the Sabbath: with thought.

To Remember and Forget

By remembering the World to Come during our earthly sojourn, we will forget this world when we get to the World to Come. Similarly, by remembering the Sabbath during the six workdays, we are able to forget the workdays during the Sabbath.

Far and Near

In God, even what seems contradictory is true. Similarly, in the Sabbath, we revere the Sabbath by repelling all work and also by remembering to rest.

Lost and Found

During the entire week, we meet up with spiritual levels and holy sparks. They slip through our fingers as we focus on our physical accomplishments. Then on the Sabbath, we seek that which was lost, and we return the lost objects to their rightful owners.

We Were Sent

The Sabbath helps us remember why we were sent to this world, and this is strongest at the moment of birth and at the moment of death.

The Head

Surely, what is most important to you is
what you think about all the time. It is
the head, and the body follows.
The Sabbath is the head for all
the six workdays and is what
we think about all the time.

Deep Desire

Deep in every Jewish heart is the desire to
be with God. But the earthly desires, an
illusion by comparison, surround the heart.
On the Sabbath, the true desire blossoms,
and all the others fall away.

Forgetting

By forgetting the work of the weekdays,
we remember the Sabbath.
Man sleeps, but his heart is awake.

Humility

The Sabbath inspires two measures of humility. We are humble because we have just departed from the slavery of the weekdays. Then by realizing the expansive freedom of the Sabbath, we feel even smaller in comparison.

Love

Love helps us remember. That memory, however, is mixed with the love for ourselves. But remembering from awe and respect is purer. The Sabbath, too, is remembered with love and awe by observing its rest.

Our Work

During the six workdays when the work of our hands and strength are most important, we forget our Creator. On the Sabbath, the heavens open, and we witness the Creation.

wisdom

With wisdom, one can discern and separate good from evil, as entangled as they may be. Once separated, the good can be improved to perfection. Similarly, one must first separate the Sabbath from the weekdays, in a total and absolute way. Then, he can sanctify and bask in its light.

---

awareness

One who realizes his arrogance and, therefore, humbles himself has the energy to be humbled to the very earth. Similarly, those who realize their arrogance during the six workdays merit the humility of the Sabbath.

---

memory

Sabbath takes one from his materialistic pursuits and allows him to return to God's service. And from each Sabbath, a memory ought to remain for each of the workdays.

wine

The workdays are ruled by logic and follow
a set of laws. We, therefore, use wine in
the kiddush ceremony consecrating
the Sabbath; we put aside the workday
knowledge with the power of wine, then
the Tree of Life of the Sabbath takes over.

Not Enough

It is not enough to receive the holiness of
the Sabbath, but to remember, to take
it with us into the weekdays. Thus,
although a day of pure spirit, the three
meals are part of Sabbath's honor.
To infuse the physical with spirit
and always remember God's presence.

God's Names

There are two names of God in every
created thing: the name spelled yod and
heh, and vov and heh, implying the
essential becoming. That name is higher
than the Creation. Then there is the name
E-lo-him, implying master and ruler.
Thus, by witnessing the Sabbath,
we declare God's mastery of the world.

one whole

The universe has three aspects: space, time, and spirit, which are as three entwined strands of a rope. Parts of the strands are revealed, while others are concealed. The revealed is of the earth, the concealed of heaven. Together they make one whole. Our Sabbath together with God's make one whole.

---

to search

A servant watches the treasure house of the king, while his son the prince can enter and search it. The first is to observe the Sabbath; the second is to remember the Sabbath.

---

from then

Decreed from the days of Creation, the exile of Egypt was destined to happen from the six workdays. The Exodus, too, was destined from the first Sabbath.

God's Name

Sabbath is the name of God, and we always remember Him. And He always remembers us, and that is the spark of divine spirituality in each of us.

Watchful

Remember. Observe and be watchful that you don't forget the Sabbath.

9

Perfection

complete

All creations of the six workdays need to be repaired; they are imperfect. The Sabbath, however, is complete, not only for itself, but it lends completeness to the entire Creation.

---

finished work

When work is done, a spirit rests on it, and it becomes more than the sum of its parts. It enjoys a special spiritual charm that causes man to find joy in it. Sabbath is wholly filled with that spirit and needs no work, and it is, therefore, forbidden.

The Will

There is the will and the act: the will is the
Sabbath; the act is the six workdays.

Escape

Sabbath is the complete escape from
all that is "wrong" with the world.
It is the most complete and
perfect time that we have.

Without Limit

The weekdays, filled with physical activity,
are limited as all physical things are.
Sabbath, on the other hand, is infinite,
just as the soul is.

Infinity

Every created thing is limited within its
boundaries. That is true for appearances.
But their inner portion is without limit and
is infinite. We learn that from the Sabbath.
On that day, we see past the surface
to the very edge of the universe.

Great Desire

On the Sabbath, there is a yearning in man's heart to divine inspiration. Similarly, there is great heavenly desire for the Jewish people.

A Prayer

The praise of God rises from His accomplishments: the six workdays, and all that was created and continues to be done. Sabbath, on the other hand, is a prayer.

One

The world was created with ten commands. The wicked are connected to the plurality of the commands. But the righteous connect to the commander, the Creator. They make from the ten, one.

Alphabet

"*Vayevorech es* . . . And He blessed the seventh day." "*Es*" is composed of the first and the last letter of the Hebrew alphabet, aleph and tav; they were all used to create the world. Sabbath raises them up high.

The Ladder

The connection of heaven and earth, the soul and the body, the Sabbath to the weekdays are as a ladder leading from the deepest pit to the highest landing. If one is lifted up, however, he no longer needs the ladder.

Beyond Sin

The action of the Jewish people was fixed at Mount Sinai and then ruined with the worship of the Golden Calf. On the Sabbath, however, they can again attain the highest level.

as new

Even if one does not rectify his errors
during the six workdays, the Sabbath
can bring him renewal. And with it,
all his days are as new.

---

without doubt

One needs faith during the weekdays that
the curse makes way for the blessing.
When the Sabbath comes, it is blessed,
without doubt, and needs no faith.

---

after sin

After sin, holiness is not as accessible
as before. But the Sabbath, untouchable
by sin, is still there in all its splendor
and holiness. It is always perfect.

family

The Jewish people passed through three levels. They were God's daughter, receiving freedom at the Exodus; they were the sister at Mount Sinai, conversing with God; and they were mother, repenting the sin of idolatry, creating a totally new path. Sabbath is formed of all three. The Sabbath of Creation and the Exodus is "daughter." Receiving the Torah at Mount Sinai on the Sabbath is "sister." And the Sabbath of the World to Come is "mother," fixing all sinful acts forever.

---

choice

One ought not serve God out of habit, but each time with choice, decision, and determination. Then the doors open, and that is the Sabbath.

Dust and Ashes

Abraham's descendants were blessed with two qualities: to be as the dust of the earth and as ashes. The dust of the earth is the foundation for all building efforts; and ashes are a result of a consuming fire, total negation of the vanities we inherit from other cultures. Those who humble themselves and negate the power plays of the workdays are worthy to receive the Sabbath.

Unity

From God comes unity, and wholeness, and that is the Sabbath.

One Whole

The entire week we attempt to raise our inanimate, vegetative, and animal natures to higher levels. The Sabbath arrives and completes our work. We become one whole man.

glimpse

The World to Come is without work whatsoever. It is total and complete rest and basking in the light of God. And the Sabbath, as a glimpse of that world, is to be free of any work, plan, desire, or waiting for work: to forget completely and absolutely the need and pleasure of work, of doing, and of physical effort.

---

intended

The image of the intended world descends from heaven with the arrival of the Sabbath.

---

connected

How can the mundane, material workdays be connected to the Sabbath? How can they also share in its spiritual gifts? By using the work of the workdays and preparing for the Sabbath. Similarly, the World to Come would be remote and untouchable but for our preparing for it in our lifetime.

Evil Follows

Evil follows the good and complete.
Thus, as the Creation became complete,
evil was not far behind. It, therefore,
needs protection. When we remember
the perfect Creation on the Sabbath,
it needs our protection,
and we observe the Sabbath.

To Return

The perfection of the Sabbath is to return
everything to its roots. And who can do it?
Those who have access to the roots:
the Jewish people who were
given the Sabbath.

True Wisdom

There are thirty-two paths of wisdom,
half from thought and half from action.
Sixteen of them are from the brain,
and the other sixteen are from
the physical body. Action must
follow thinking: to remember
the Sabbath and to observe
the Sabbath.

Low and High

There is the lower and the higher level
of the righteous. The lower *tzadik* sees
all that needs fixing in himself and
in others. The higher *tzadik* sees
the goodness inherent in everything.
And that is the Sabbath.

Integrate

Sabbath is the integrative factor of diverse
thoughts, talents, and potential energy
that one feels during the weekdays.

Null and Void

The body, although physical, can be
unified. But the true unity belongs to
the soul of man. And by negating
the body to the soul, it becomes
the soul's reflection. Similarly,
the six days can be unified,
yet they reach the highest unity
if negated to the Sabbath.

pleasure

Physical desires and pleasures have their roots in the highest spheres. And those who keep them from being defiled are rewarded with the pleasure of the Sabbath.

The Haughty

God lowers the haughty in order to raise them up. He lowers during the six workdays, to raise on the Sabbath.

Two Hearts

Our heart is made of two hearts: the wise and the foolish. Both must be united in the service of God. And they are, through prayer and hard work. Our soul, on the other hand, is unified and enlightened, and infuses our heart with light. The six workdays represent the heart, and the Sabbath represents our soul.

Above Logic

Even if logically there is no chance of
spiritual success, one must rise above logic.
He must negate his logic to God's will
so that the illogical can happen.
Logic rules in the six workdays.
Sabbath towers above it all.

Infinite

While the workdays are only six and
are limited, the Sabbath is one and
is infinite. If we bind them together,
we can find the infinite even in the six.

The Inside

The husk of each thing is struggle and
hiddenness, while the inside is harmony
and revelation. The husk is the six
workdays, and the inside is the Sabbath.

The center

The focus of all of man's limbs is
the covenant, the word of God, especially
the circumcision. The focus of all
of man's days is the Sabbath.
It is the center of the spiritual circle.

Soul and Body

There are two major aspects of the
Sabbath: to remember the creation and
to remember the Exodus. God's day of rest
is for the soul: it is the elevation of
the spirit. Freedom from slavery is for
the body: complete rest and recuperation.

Perfect

Although the natural world is imperfect,
its plan was perfect. And although our
deeds are imperfect, they are perfect
in our imagination. The Sabbath is
the imagined world of perfection,
and all work is excluded.

Raised Up High

The workdays are of this world, while the
Sabbath is totally removed and is from
the world of the spirit. Then how can man,
a creature of material, connect to
the Sabbath? It is with the Exodus
that the Jewish people
were raised higher to that realm.

Sand

The sea is the wisdom of the world and
is protected by the sand, *chol*, which are
the Jewish people. And through them,
the entire world receives wisdom.
The workdays, *chol*, protect the Sabbath,
when we yearn for the Sabbath in them.
Then all the world receives
the blessings of the Sabbath.

Heavenly Day

Each day of the week has a heavenly twin.
We must work to raise the level of
each day to its spiritual counterpart;
except for the Sabbath,
which is the heavenly day itself.

Desolation

The world started with desolation and ended with creation. Similarly, each time there would be renewal, there is a return to nothingness. This is reflected in the life of man. He is born with the desire for evil and then receives his inclination to do good. Similarly, the week starts with nothing and ends with the Sabbath.

The Peak

Whatever might have been created on the Sabbath was quickly created on the sixth day, and this includes man, the highest of the earthly creatures. His soul, however, reached its peak on the Sabbath. Similarly, the collective soul of the Jewish people also reached its peak on the Sabbath, the day that the Torah was given on Mount Sinai.

The Donkey

"Your ox and donkey . . . ," the physical part of you, also, must rest on the Sabbath. And although the body cannot rest during this lifetime, in the World to Come it, too, will have complete rest.

Numbers

What is a large number? It is a collection
of many single numbers. And being
separated, they are in danger of harm
by evil. But united, they are safe.
The six workdays, too, are in danger,
till the Sabbath comes and makes one
of them. All hearts unite with God.

Earth and Heaven

On the earth as in heaven. As he prepares
the Sabbath, man receives the Sabbath
of heaven. As his soul yearns for heaven,
so does he receive a loftier soul
from that very place.

One at a Time

Evil has the power to knock down
the good one at a time. On the Sabbath,
all gather and become united,
and evil has no power against them.

Start

Every new thing must start with
the Sabbath; there, it connects to the root
of Creation and finds its spiritual life.

Level Ground

The six workdays are like the repentant:
hills and valleys, ups and downs,
sin and repentance. The Sabbath is like
the *tzadik*, the righteous who steadily
and firmly walk on level ground.

Doubly Perfect

Everything about the Sabbath is doubled,
bringing the other-worldly holiness into
the physical realm. It allows us to perfect
even our flawed, imperfect nature.

In the End

In the end, all will be happy to see the
results of observing the commandments.
And this is the reason for the true joy
on Sabbath, as it is a fraction of
the World to Come.

Energy

Each day God renews the world with
the energy of the Creation.
Sabbath itself, however, is that energy.

Level by Level

The most material level is bodily action.
With the arrival of the Sabbath
Friday night, action is elevated by resting.
Speech is more spiritual and is elevated on
the morning of the Sabbath.
And finally, the highest of man's attributes,
thinking, is also elevated on
Sabbath afternoon.
Thus, he reaches out for perfection.

Sensitivity

Ever since the Jewish people heard
the Ten Commandments on Mount Sinai,
their hearts are sensitive to the facts
of Creation and are thus the witnesses
for the Sabbath.

Positive and Negative

The positive commandments of the Torah
elevate the spiritual level of the soul.
The negative commandments keep
the arteries open to spread the spiritual
throughout. Similarly, one who observes
the Sabbath creates a vessel, and
by remembering, is then filled
with perfection.

As Before

The goal of the Creation was man.
Therefore, he precedes every being;
although he was created last,
after everything. From all the days
of the week, only Sabbath remained in
the original state, as God's plan before
Creation. It is the day when man, too,
can rediscover his perfection.

future, now

With God, the future, the past, and
the present are all here and now.
Thus, in observing God's commandments,
we connect to all dimensions of space
and time. We fix the past, grasp
the present, and guarantee our future.
The Sabbath, too, is from the World to
Come and descends to fill our life with
a glorious future in the present.

---

seven virtues

Twice in one's lifetime, one realizes that
he does not contribute one iota to
his being alive: at birth and at death.
He totally negates all his seven virtues
to the one and only God.
And that is the Sabbath.

---

protection

When man protects his inner holiness
from defilement by material exteriors,
it will shine outward and make holy
even his physical garments.
That inner holiness is the Sabbath.

Perfection

singing

Our world is a mixture of good and evil,
and when separated there is rejoicing
and song. These are the songs that
we sing during the three meals
in honor of the Sabbath.

Transformation

God gave us the power to lift our errant
life and reconnect it to its roots of holiness
and infinite blessing. We can reconnect
our cursed, physical, and lowly workdays
to their roots, too. And that is the Sabbath.

---

complete unity

In observing God's commandments,
it is not only necessary to unite all
of one's limbs, not only to unite
his individuality to the collective soul of
the Jewish people, but to connect it
to generations, from the first to the last.
That is the way to observe the Sabbath.

Master

The Jewish people are asked to witness that God created the world. And they do so by helping others realize it, too. Sabbath, however, is above and beyond the Creation, the becoming and being of all, revealed only to those who are ready.

Interconnected

Just as the six workdays need the Sabbath, the Sabbath needs the six workdays, too.

One Pursuit

The only activity that man does should be merely, only, and exclusively the Sabbath.

Divine Kernel

The divine kernel and truth that God placed in every creature is beyond reach of defilement by sin, untouchable by material meddling.
And that is the Sabbath.

Greater

God's creation of the universe in six days
was truly awesome. Yet, His day of rest
following was greater still.

Turning Away

We can either turn away from or turn
toward God, while God faces us all
the time. When we turn away from
our physical work, we receive
the Sabbath face to face.

Confusion

Although the nations have knowledge,
confusion misleads them. The Jewish
people, however, are connected to
the clarity of the Tree of Life and help
the nations sort out their confusions, too.

Garments

Before we clothe ourselves in the holy
garments of the Sabbath, we need to
remove the workday garments. And thus,
we purify ourselves for the Sabbath.

from aleph

Sabbath has to be observed with thought,
speech, and action. And the perfection
of the Sabbath needs to he taken into
the workdays—from aleph, the first letter,
till tav, the last letter.

---

feet

Just as the feet ought to follow the head,
so, too, the workdays are the feet
of the Sabbath.

---

within

Perfection is unchanging and is within
the temporary and changing nature
of things. It is there, and we could find it.
Thus, we could find the Sabbath.

---

forty-nine

The Jewish people left the forty-nine
Egyptian gates of defilement. Their heart
then opened to the forty-nine gates
of purity and understanding. They can,
therefore, see through the hiddenness
and witness the Sabbath.

The Essence

Garments can be changed. Sabbath, on the other hand, becomes part of man's heart.

One Name

During the workdays, the Jewish people have names; they are not yet on the highest level of unity. On the Sabbath, they have one name, God's name, which unites them totally and absolutely.

The Crown

Man must attempt to place as many precious stones in the king's crown while he has time. He does this during the workdays, and the finished crown is the Sabbath.

Reasons

Love for a reason is in the measure of the reason. Love for no reason has no measure and is infinite. Thus, Sabbath's observance is from sundown to sundown, yet it is without limit and we add on to its beginning and end.

Great Loss

On the Sabbath, when the elevated soul enters us, we realize how much bigger we could have been. And that hurts, and we sigh, "Woe is to our loss!"

Journeys

There are many journeys and wanderings a human being has to make before he arrives at his destination. They are the workdays, and finally there is the complete uninterrupted rest of Sabbath.

Preparing

At a future time, God's kingdom will be revealed in full clarity. Now, however, His servants prepare the world for that event. Just as our preparations during the six workdays allow the Sabbath to be revealed.

union

In each of the six days of Creation,
another aspect of the universe
was created. No two days are alike,
and what one lacks, the other fulfills.
Then came the Sabbath, and with it
the union of all the days and
their particular attributes.

---

stirring

Observing the commandments with action
stirs man more than without action.
Still, Sabbath is higher than all of them.

---

song

On the day of Sabbath, when the entire
Creation is united, a song resounds
from all creatures.

---

joseph

The twelve tribes are set for action and lift
the spirit of the workdays, while Joseph,
the righteous one, is the Sabbath.

Healing

The commandments heal the body's flaws
during the weekdays; while the Torah gives
light for the soul on the Sabbath.

Our Faith

God's providence is recognized according
to the strength of our faith in Him.
And that faith is necessary to overcome
the falsehood of the world, the six
workdays. On the Sabbath,
the truth is revealed.

The Exodus

Six days passed from the time the Jewish
people were released from Egypt.
On the seventh day, the Red Sea split,
and they were totally free. Similarly,
there are six workdays, liberating
the faithful one day at a time,
followed by the Sabbath
and total liberation.

very high

Someday, all will realize their level
of spiritual attainment. At present,
however, it is impossible to know,
it is so high. And that is the Sabbath.

---

unnatural

There were forty-eight journeys from
Egypt to the promised land, desolate and
uninhabitable places. Similarly, there are
in each of our lives forty-eight epochs
and forty-eight Sabbaths throughout the
lunar year. In sum, there are places, times,
and souls that do not adhere to the rules
of nature. And that is the Sabbath.

---

pure enjoyment

There are elements and compounds
with by-products. The six workdays
are combined with good and evil.
Sabbath is the element, the foundation,
and is pure. Thus, if it is enjoyed,
one can assume that it is pure joy.

1/60

The Sabbath is but one-sixtieth of
the World to Come. And the entire
lifetime is a Sabbath eve,
preparing for the Sabbath.

---

incomplete

Really no one could experience the
World to Come unless he has entirely
elevated every part of his body. When the
Sabbath arrives, however, and man drops
all his work, although unfinished, God, too,
allows him to experience the
World to Come, although incomplete.

---

weaving

During the six workdays, man must sift,
separate, and find the kernel of divine
spirituality in each thing. Then, he
connects all those bits and weaves
a complete revelation of God's kingdom.
And that is the Sabbath.

Reward

The wicked chooses the lusts and pleasures
of this fragmented world, and it
is considered his reward. The righteous,
on the other hand, wants only to escape
this dimension and dwell in
the inner realm: the six workdays
and the Sabbath.

Adam's Sin

Although Adam sinned, the Sabbath
protected him. No evil has the power
to spoil its holiness.

New Day

Each day, the Creation is renewed.
Today is the day, new in every way.
And on the Sabbath day, when all
of the Creation returns to its origins
and roots, all are uplifted
and are blessed.

Hairs

The path of evil is but a hair's breadth.
The wicked can't even overcome
the first hair. The righteous overcome
hair after hair, totaling a large mountain.
And for nations, their souls unite
and are called the children of God.
And that is their name during the Sabbath.

Truth

The Jewish people wait all week for
the Sabbath, to be near truth and
to straighten their crooked hearts
to that truth.

10

Peace

pleasing the king

Nature is bound, forced to do what it does. On Sabbath, though, it desires to please the king and feels happy and at peace.

---

certainty

Man's life has many moments of uncertainty. They are like shaky planks under his feet. He needs to connect them to the infinite, to the Sabbath. Then he can walk safely and arrive at his destination.

king of peace

Every created being has its balanced
opposition, and it is, therefore, without
peace. This is true of every single number.
God gives life, and all turn to Him
to receive it. He is, thus, the king of peace.

---

oneness

The Sabbath is connected to the root
of oneness. She is, therefore, the queen
mother of all time, and in her all time
finds unity and peace.

---

within the husk

The creative force in each being is
the word of God. It is surrounded
by a husk, a material shell, concealing it.
All joy comes from the inner light;
all depression from the husk.
The six workdays are the entanglement
of the light and the husk. On Sabbath,
the husk falls away, divine light is revealed,
and all depression is banished.

Peace

With Tranquility

Holiness in man's heart is thoroughly covered and concealed. It is revealed with great effort and battle during the six workdays. On the Sabbath, it is revealed with peace and tranquility.

The Peace of Holiness

When are the Jewish people at peace? When holiness is revealed. On the Sabbath, with holiness descending, they are at peace.

Even on the Weekdays

If we prepare and are ready for the Sabbath peace, then we also merit to feel its tranquility during the workdays.

Quiet

The admixture of good and evil is in turmoil and in a state of chaos. Moving away from evil and doing good instead, man reaches tranquility. That is the Sabbath peace.

peace at last

With Sabbath's arrival, the spirit is no longer concealed by the imperfections of the material world. A wholeness appears, and all is at peace.

---

time

The Jewish people were redeemed from Egypt physically and spiritually. Time is redeemed both physically and spiritually on the Sabbath. That is true peace.

---

has nothing

Who has peace? Not he who is impressed and runs after riches; not he who is jealous of another's accomplishments. It is he who nullifies his being to God, realizing that he possesses nothing and that all is from God. When? On the Sabbath.

Refuge of peace

The refuge of God is hidden within nature,
and the Jewish people yearn to reveal it.
Their yearning gives the energy to reveal
it, and all the world sees its truth.
And they get covered with
the tent of peace: the Sabbath.

Whole peace

No pleasure can be enjoyed on earth
without some flaw. With the Torah,
however, completeness is attained.
The Sabbath, spreading its tent of peace,
allows us to enjoy it fully.

Witnessing

The Jewish people are God's witnesses,
and all their actions, speech, and thought
are focused to that end. And everything
one spoke about in the workdays, he raises
to the level of witnessing, and from them
all a tent of peace is fashioned.

The Kohen

The Jewish people need to negate themselves and attach themselves to the *Kohanim*—priests who are the root and channel for their blessings. Similarly, man must move and cleave to the Sabbath.

Life and Knowledge

The workdays have the confusion of the Tree of Knowledge, evening and morning, darkness and light. The Sabbath is the Tree of Life and decisively overpowers knowledge on the Sabbath day. And that is peace.

Peace at the Root

The root of the blessing, before it is clothed in material, is inactive and at peace. It possesses peace, and it is the Sabbath.

The Collective

God desires each individual to negate
himself to the collective soul of
Klal Yisroel, the congregation of Israel,
to draw the Sabbath into the weekdays
and transform them.

Becoming One

God is the absolute singularity. Then how
does plurality exist? It is only in that
all creatures negate themselves to God
that they exist. All negate their work,
deeds, and accomplishments to
the Sabbath; the total and absolute peace.

Only Kindness

While the individual may survive
being ruled with judgment, the collective
would never survive. Therefore,
the Sabbath, in whom all are united,
is pure loving kindness.

Evidence

The work of the six workdays is
an investigation, seeking and discovering
evidence, followed by the Sabbath:
the final and definite witnessing.

Rest in God

A creature is active and moving and not
at rest. It rests in being null and void in
God's presence. That is Sabbath's peace.

Inner Peace

The face-to-face contact of a creature and
its creator, the bit of vitality infused in it,
is its wholeness and completeness
and is the peace present in all things.

Right and Left

The entire Creation is united in God and
is at peace. Still, there are contradictions,
day and night, right and left. Man is pulled
once this way and once that way during the
six workdays. And then comes the Sabbath,
and all are united as one in peace.

working for peace

In the six days of Creation, there was an infinite desire to reach the peace and restfulness of the Sabbath. That desire was entwined in work. Thus, work became the foundation for the Sabbath peace.

awe

In human nature, if one loves, he does not fear; and if one fears, he really doesn't love. In God, however, those two contradictions unite, in awe of Him. And that is true peace.

peace at end

Disagreement for God's sake brings peace at the end. Similarly, each day is distinct and individually important and disagrees with an aspect of one of the other days. And it is all done to reach out to the spiritual essence in God. Therefore, they all unite in the Sabbath.

Through Work

With man's pure desire to move through the workdays, he reaches the Sabbath's peace. Through the wisdom of work, one reaches intelligence and understanding. That longing and desire brings the Sabbath peace.

Waiting

Just as we as individuals wait for the Sabbath, so, too, the entire Creation waits for it.

Bring Near

Those who seek peace can help bring others close to God, even those who are not worthy. And that can be done on Sabbath.

Benefit

Struggle with the forces of evil is beneficial during the six workdays. Then peace is attained on the Sabbath.

both

The Sabbath has both the strength and
security of the Torah of Moses, and
the tent of peace of Aaron.

---

watching

Just as the person watches the Sabbath,
the Sabbath watches him, too.

---

permanent peace

Man waits all week for the peacefulness
and tranquility of the Sabbath. It is not
a burden to him that he abandons all
his physical pursuits. On the contrary,
it is his permanent mind and place.
It is his very life and vitality.

---

ignorant

In every created thing there is God's
desire, His joy and pleasure, unknown
and unknowable. Although ignorant of
the divine purpose, nevertheless,
we must guard the Godly core.
And that is the peace within the Sabbath.

True Rest

There are two types of rest. Man rests when he has nothing to do. He also rests after his strenuous work to finish a project. That is a peaceful rest. That is where he wants to be: all finished and resting peacefully. That is the Sabbath.

Divine Peace

Imagine the level of peace attainable on the Sabbath, being God's day of rest—infinite and divine.

Tent of Peace

Sabbath is a tent of peace, and all rest under it and experience its peacefulness.

All Work

Man has much spiritual work still undone. How can he ever complete it? When he discards all his physical work with the advent of the Sabbath, God immediately completes all his work for him.

Dust of the Earth

The Jewish people are likened to the dust of the earth. To them, everything returns, and everything grows. And those who can humble themselves become part of this wonderful dust. That dust is the peacefulness of the Sabbath.

Looking for Peace

Those who are totally peaceful during the Sabbath look for peace and goodness in everything and make those virtues grow in their hearts.

Heaven and Earth

The human body and its six workdays are the earth; the soul and the Sabbath are the heavens. On the Sabbath, we finally realize that God made both of them.

Four Corners

The Jewish people were given the power to take the four farthest corners of the universe and unite them as one. That is the power of their Sabbath.

sealed

The gifts of God, as the land of Israel
and the Sabbath, are sealed with a seal
within a seal. And when the chaff
falls away, then the secret is revealed.

True Rest

One can achieve true rest if he remembers
where he is, when he is, and who he is.
This can be achieved on the Sabbath.

One Letter

All the letters of the Hebrew alphabet are
in heaven, from aleph till tav, and they are
on the earth, too. With the combination,
mixing, and compounding of the letters,
the universe was built. Their inner essence,
though, is God's name, one letter of which
is the life of all. Thus, although much work
is needed during the workdays,
the Sabbath is nothing but peace.
Not another thing needs to be done.

Traditional Sabbath Observance

It is a firmly held belief among all traditional men and women of the Jewish faith that the Sabbath is the seventh day of the week since Creation. The first man and woman, Adam and Eve, experienced it and taught it to their children. Finally, with the appearance of Abraham, the Sabbath became firmly established as the holy day of the Hebrew tribes. Continuing with Isaac, Jacob, and his descendants, the Sabbath played a major role in the liberation of the Israelites from Egyptian slavery and their settlement in the Land of Canaan, Eretz Israel.

The Sabbath is observed from nightfall to nightfall, the night being the traditional start of the Jewish day. Out of reverence for its holiness, we are obliged to add on to the Sabbath both when it starts and when it ends. We, therefore, complete all our preparations for the Sabbath 18 minutes before sunset on Friday afternoon and end its observance no sooner than the sighting of three medium stars in the evening sky on

Saturday night. (Approximately 45, 50, or 60 minutes after sunset.)

It is customary to do some physical work on Friday in preparation for the Sabbath, such as sweeping or vacuuming, polishing one's shoes, or other similar preparations. This, as well as bathing and dressing in clean clothing and tidying up the house, enhances the respect for the Sabbath.

If possible, a table should be covered with a cloth, and two whole loaves of bread or challah, large or small, also covered, should be placed on it. Then, two candles in holders and a cup for the kiddush prayer should also be placed on the table.

The woman of the household, or in her absence the man, lights the candles 18 minutes before sunset and does the following:

Light the candles. Then cover the eyes and recite the blessing.

Blessed are You, God, our God, King of the universe, Who sanctified us with His commandments and has commanded us to kindle the light of the Sabbath.

It is a fitting and propitious time, while covering the eyes, to pray for loved ones to mature spiritually. Others recite the following prayer:

May it be Your will, God, my God and the God of my forefathers, that you show favor to me, my husband, my sons, my daughters, my father, my mother, and all my relatives. And grant us all and all of Israel a good and long life. Remember us with a beneficent memory

Traditional Sabbath Observance

and blessing. Consider us with a consideration of salvation and compassion. Bless us with great blessing. Make our household complete. Cause Your presence to dwell among us. Give me the privilege to raise children and grandchildren who are wise and understanding, who love and fear God, who are people of truth, holy offspring, to God bound, who illuminate the world with Torah and good deeds, and with all sorts of work in the service of God. Please hear my supplication at this time, in the merit of Sarah, Rebecca, Rachel, and Leah, our mothers, and light our lamp so that it does not extinguish forever and ever. And let Your countenance shine, and we will be saved. Amen.

Following Sabbath evening services, a cup is filled with wine (or grape juice), and kiddush is recited.

(Silently—And there was evening and there was morning.)

The sixth day. Thus, the heavens and the earth were finished and all their array. On the seventh day, God completed His work that He had done, and He abstained on the seventh day from all His work that He had done. And God blessed the seventh day and hallowed it, because on it He abstained from all His work that God created to make.

By your leave, my masters, rabbis, and teachers.

Blessed are You, God, our God, King of the universe, Who creates the fruit of the vine.

Blessed are You, God, our God, King of the universe, Who has sanctified us with His commandments, took pleasure in us, and with love and favor gave us His holy Sabbath as a heritage, a remembrance of creation. For that day is the prologue to the convocations, a memorial to the Exodus from Egypt. (For us did you choose and us did you sanctify from all the nations.) And Your holy Sabbath, with love and favor, did you give us as a heritage. Blessed are You, God, Who sanctifies the Sabbath.

Drink from the wine, and share with the assembled. Wash the hands, hold the two breads, and say, Blessed are You, God, our God, King of the universe, Who brings forth bread from the earth. Then, the Sabbath meal is eaten, including at least one thing in honor of the Sabbath. Two other meals are eaten during the day.

When the Sabbath is over, the *Havdalah* is recited.

Behold! God is my salvation, I shall trust and not fear—for God is my might and my praise—God—and He was a salvation for me. You can draw water with joy, from the springs of salvation. Salvation is God's, upon Your people is Your blessing, selah. God, Master of legions, is with us, a stronghold for us is the God of Jacob, selah. God, Master of legions, praised is the man who trusts in You. God save! May the King answer us on the day we call. For the Jews, there was light, gladness, joy, and honor—so may it be for us. I will raise the cup of salvation, and I shall invoke the name of God.

By your leave, my masters and teachers.

Blessed are You, God, our God, King of the universe, Who creates the fruit of the vine.

Blessed are You, God, our God, King of the universe, Who creates species of fragrance.

(Smell the spices.)

Blessed are You, God, our God, King of the universe, Who created the illumination of the fire.

(Hold the fingers up to the flame to see the reflected light.)

Blessed are You, God, our God, King of the universe, Who separates between the holy and the secular, between light and darkness, between Israel and the nations, between the seventh day and the six days of labor. Blessed are You, God, Who separates between the holy and the secular.

Drink the cup of wine, extinguish the flame of the candles with the wine.

It is also traditional to eat another meal at the conclusion of the Sabbath, the *Melaveh Malkah*, to accompany the Sabbath Queen and take its holiness with us as we begin the next week of work.

About the Author

Moshe A. Braun is director of Hope Educational Services, servicing communities with educational innovations. He also directs the Free Jewish University, a Torah outreach program for college-age youth. A Holocaust survivor who has written and lectured on the subject at college campuses, he is also one of the pioneers in popularized Chasidic ideas and thought through lectures and published articles. Braun has written more than ten books, including *The Talking B'somim Box* (1990), *Leap of Faith* (1992), *The Magic Comb* (1993), *The Jewish Holy Days* (1996), *Pointing the Way: Spiritual Insights from the Sfas Emes,* and *The Heschel Tradition: The Life and Teachings of Rabbi Abraham Joshua Heschel of Apt* (1997). He currently resides in New York with his wife and children.